The Films of
Joan Crawford

A typical Crawford glamor shot of the mid-1930s

The Films of Joan Crawford

by Lawrence J. Quirk

The Citadel Press   Secaucus, New Jersey

Third paperbound printing, 1973
Copyright © 1968 by Lawrence J. Quirk
All rights reserved
Published by The Citadel Press
A division of Lyle Stuart Inc.
120 Enterprise Avenue, Secaucus, N.J. 07094
In Canada: George J. McLeod Limited
73 Bathurst St., Toronto 2B, Ontario
Manufactured in the United States of America
ISBN 0-8065-0008-5
Designed by Al Swiller

Photograph Acknowledgments

Metro-Goldwyn-Mayer, Inc., Norman Kaphan, Dore Freeman; Universal Pictures, Inc., Milt Livingston; Columbia Pictures, Inc., John Newfield and Hortense Schorr; Warner Brothers-Seven Arts, Inc., Wynn Loewenthal; UPI, Pete Sansone; Twentieth Century-Fox Film Corp., Sonia Wolfson; Martin Quigley, Jr., Albert B. Manski, Frank Leyendecker, Ray Gain, James D. Armour, Gerald D. McDonald, Eric Benson, John and Lem Amero, and last, but far from least, the late Jerry Asher.

This book is dedicated to
my uncle, James R. Quirk (1884–1932)
editor and publisher of Photoplay Magazine
in the days when it was proud and beautiful

And to
my friends in foul, as well as fair, weather:
Margaret Connery Quirk
James E. Runyan
Damon Fenner

CONTENTS

Joan Crawford:
The Actress and the Woman

Joan Crawford is a typically American film star. She is American in that she projects enterprise, resiliency, and drive in her performances. She is also American in that she hangs on to her gains. She has been a leading cinema personality for forty-three years through eighty films—and for ten of those years she has also been a successful businesswoman.

Among her on-screen images: the shopgirl who aspires to better things; the ambitious prostitute who seeks respectability—and the man to help her get it; the lady-thief who assumes the manners and mores of the aristocrats she is fleecing; the stenographer who wants to rise from a drab life on a ladder of men; the stranded carnival girl who seeks a haven; the man-shark who steals the husbands of less aggressive women.

Miss Crawford is also expert at portraying screen characters in the throes of romantic passion. She has gone colorfully mad because her love was not returned. She has been hurt because she chose to love a heel. She has been a factory girl entranced by a seedy chiseler. She has been a hard-boiled, emotionally insulated stage star softened by love.

Other Crawford roles: A physically afflicted woman who must learn the rules of life and love from the ground up. An unloving wife who prizes her well-kept house above her husband. An overly indulgent mother who makes an emotional monster of her child. A rich widow with a penchant for handsome beach bums. A lonely spinster who marries too hastily and discovers her young husband is a psychotic. A self-centered magazine editor in love with a married man. A domineering, sadistic head nurse in a mental hospital. *And* an ex-mental hospital inmate suspected of axe murders.

In the 1925–1927 period, she was little more than a big-eyed MGM ingénue who won Charleston contests in her off-hours. By 1928 she was box office. By 1939 she had developed first-class acting skills. And in 1945 she won an Academy Award, followed in subsequent years by a number of "Best Actress" Oscar nominations.

In 1938 she was labeled "box-office poison." From 1943 to 1945 she was out of a job. She weathered other career slumps in 1948 and 1954. She was divorced thrice, widowed once—and has not tried marriage again in nearly a decade. Along the way, she has raised four adopted children to adulthood.

There are six periods in the Crawford film career. The jazz baby and peppy ingénue (1925–1929); the modern girl, languorous, cynical, world-weary (1930–1933); the sophisticated, hollow-cheeked clotheshorse (1934–1940); the accomplished dramatic actress (1941–1952); the seasoned, adaptable veteran (1953–1957); and the star emeritus who divides her time between film roles and a New York business career (1958 to date).

Born on March 23, 1908, in San Antonio, Texas, she was christened Lucille LeSueur. Her parents were divorced when she was a baby, and her father disappeared from her life. Her mother then married a vaudeville theatre manager named Cassin, and the family (she had an older brother, Hal) moved to Lawton, Oklahoma. There Lucille adopted the name Billie Cassin. She learned a lot about backstage theatre life at this time, and her interest in dancing sprang from watching the vaudeville performers do their routines.

Billie formed a deep attachment to her stepfather, but he too disappeared from her life when her mother divorced him in 1915. They were now living in a cheap Kansas City hotel, and Mrs. Cassin went to work in a laundry. The family was ensconced in some rooms behind it. At nearby St.

With her brother Hal LeSueur in childhood

Agnes Convent, Billie did menial work in exchange for lessons. The better-heeled students snubbed her.

At another school, Rockingham, she again did menial work, trying hard to keep up her studies. Then her mother married for the third time, and Billie was sent to Stephens College in Columbia, Missouri. But she could not keep up scholastically, due to the meager training she had gotten between jobs at the other schools, and eventually she left. She never forgot one experience there: She had been invited to a college dance and rigged up a garish little dress ornamented with imitation lace and roses. The other girls ridiculed her appearance. Incidents of this sort strengthened her determination somehow to succeed in life.

It was now 1921. She got a job in a department store. Her first beau, one Ray Sterling, came along that year. He took her to dances where she wore the wrong clothes and made up too much and tried to ignore the opinions of others. Sterling was intelligent and well-read, though poor and young, and he inspired Billie to make something special of herself.

Blessed with hope and vitality, Billie decided that a dancing career would best further her ambitions. She began to invest most of her small salary in clothes, practiced dancing in front of full-length mirrors, and went out for amateur contests at dance halls. Then she tried out for a Katharine Emerine revue at a Kansas City hotel and was hired. But her first professional dancing job ended after a week.

More department store work followed. Then, in 1923, when she was fifteen, she won an amateur dance contest and decided to try Chicago. Katharine Emerine gave her a recommendation to Ernie Young, an agent with night club contacts. Young got her a $25-a-week job in a second-rate night spot. She proved herself a reliable performer and was moved on to a club in Detroit, the Oriole Terrace. Here she did eight routines a night with several dozen other chorus girls. During this period she set about to learn proper makeup and began to wear chic clothes. She also reverted to her original name, Lucille LeSueur.

J. J. Shubert, the Broadway impresario, was among the patrons during one of her Oriole routines. Lucille caught his eye and he offered her a job in the chorus of *Innocent Eyes*, then playing in New York.

In 1924—she was sixteen—she was holding down two jobs: one in the chorus of *Innocent Eyes*; the other filling a late-hours singing and dancing spot at Harry Richman's night club.

Then Harry Rapf, of Metro-Goldwyn-Mayer, came to New York on one of his talent-spotting trips and saw Lucille in *Innocent Eyes*. She took a screen test that proved satisfactory and in January, 1925 (still 16), she was in Hollywood under contract to MGM.

For the first year she did the usual thing: doubled for top stars, posed for cheesecake and track-running publicity stills. Finally, appeals to Rapf and others won her some bit roles.

At night she did exhibition dancing. She was particularly expert at such contemporary dance crazes as the Charleston and Black Bottom. Her vitality and uninhibited charm won her much admiration from men, among them Michael Cudahy, young scion of the Chicago meat-packing clan. Between them, she and Cudahy won dozens of Charleston trophies. But the Cudahys did not think Lucille LeSueur good enough for their son, and after an on-again-off-again period, they broke up for good.

A close friend at the time was William Haines, then a popular MGM star; their relationship was platonic. Haines encouraged Lucille's ambitions. So did Paul Bern, an MGM producer who fostered promising talent. Another early booster, cameraman

Dancing the "Black Bottom" in 1927

MG-199

Johnny Arnold, told her that she had a unique look and a face with a strong bone structure.

In Lucille LeSueur's first picture, *Pretty Ladies,* released in July, 1925, she played a chorus girl. Another "bit" followed in *The Only Thing.* In this Graustarkian romance, starring Eleanor Boardman and Conrad Nagel, Lucille played a lady of the court. A more substantial role followed in *Old Clothes,* released in November, 1925, and starring the popular child star Jackie Coogan. Jack Coogan, Sr., who guided his son's career, had noticed Lucille in one of the earlier films and had decided she would make a good foil for Jackie in the role of a homeless girl he befriends.

At this point, MGM decided that Lucille LeSueur didn't sound right for a developing screen personality. Joan Arden was one name proposed. Then the studio sponsored a contest in a film magazine and came up with Joan Crawford. "I hated the name at first," she said later. "It sounded like 'Crawfish.' Then I came to love it."

The Coogan film elicited some mild public interest in her, but she won more serious attention in *Sally, Irene and Mary,* which traced the fortunes of three chorus girls. Constance Bennett and Sally O'Neil were her co-stars. By this time, Joan had plucked her eyebrows to the latest shape. Her mouth was a red cupid's bow and her eyes were carefully made

up. She had dieted and lost weight, and had perfected a graceful walk and an erect posture.

After a small role with George K. Arthur in an inconsequential comedy, *The Boob,* released in mid-1926, she got herself a lead in *Paris,* with Charles Ray. She played an apache girl and Ray was a larking American millionaire. By now the public was vividly aware of her.

Another lead followed with Harry Langdon in *Tramp, Tramp, Tramp,* on loan to First National. She then returned to MGM and top billing in *The Taxi Dancer.* In this first of her 1927 releases she was a naïve Southern girl who falls in with New York city slickers.

Miss Crawford credits Louis B. Mayer with taking a fatherly and constructive interest in her career at this point. She says of him: "I was free to go to him for advice of any kind, any time. He was patient with people, had great judgment and didn't play games. Mr. Mayer always had a magic sense of star material, of personality. He knew how to build and protect his 'properties,' and he had a genuine love for them as people." She has consistently deplored the attacks others have made on Mayer; she claims that negative reports on him have been exaggerated and distorted.

Winners of the Wilderness, a frontier epic with Tim McCoy, was her next 1927 picture, and it did nothing for her career. Nor did her next, *The Understanding Heart,* in which she vied with a forest fire and a parachute rescue for audience attention.

The Unknown, however, was an event for her, because she was cast opposite the brilliant Lon Chaney. Of her experience with him she has written: "I became aware for the first time of the difference between standing in front of a camera and acting. Until then I had been conscious only of myself. Lon Chaney was my introduction to acting. The concentration, the complete absorption he gave to his characterization filled me with such awe I could scarcely speak to him. He was giving one of his absolutely unique characterizations in this. His arms were strapped to his sides in his role of an armless circus performer. He learned to act without hands, even to hold a cigarette between his toes. He never slipped out of character. Watching him gave me the desire to be a real actress."

At this point, Mayer decided that Joan Crawford's career would be enhanced as a "John Gilbert leading lady," and he cast her opposite this hot box-office personality of the late 1920s, the handsome actor who earlier that year had scorched the screens of America in his love scenes with Garbo. In *Twelve Miles Out,* Joan was a society girl in love with Gilbert, a rakish rumrunner. She remembers that during the picture Gilbert was so distracted by his off-screen love affair with Garbo that he could hardly concentrate and was difficult to work with.

During this period, Joan Crawford was supporting her mother and helping her brother Hal to land various studio jobs. She had acquired a house on Roxbury Drive, and a car, thanks to loans arranged for her by Mayer. She also tapered off her night life, after friends like Johnny Arnold advised her to watch her hours and public image. In 1927 and 1928 she did several pictures with her friend William Haines, including *Spring Fever* and *West Point.* In these, Haines was usually a cocky go-getter, with Miss Crawford playing the girl who tames him.

Around this time she met Douglas Fairbanks, Jr., who had been in films since 1923. It was rumored in Hollywood that Fairbanks Senior and his wife, Mary Pickford, did not approve of the romance that ensued, but the relationship proved to be constructive. The younger Fairbanks helped her obtain some polish and social poise, and she helped him reinforce his belief in his acting abilities. The opposition at Pickfair gradually subsided and they were married in 1929. Adela Rogers St. Johns, famed Hollywood chronicler, summed up the alliance succinctly: "Though it was a love match, Joan *was* anxious to better herself."

Meanwhile, Miss Crawford was getting experience in a variety of roles, including the first *Rose-Marie,* with James Murray; *Across to Singapore,* a high-seas romance with Ramon Novarro; *Law of the Range,* a Western with Tim McCoy; *Four Walls,*

in which she played moll to John Gilbert as gangster; and *Dream of Love* with Nils Asther, in which she was a peasant girl in love with a prince.

But it was *Our Dancing Daughters,* released in the fall of 1928, that made Joan Crawford a star. In this she was a dance-mad rich girl of contemporary vintage who loves and suffers. This role struck an identificatory chord with the public; her reviews were exceptionally good, and the fan letters began flooding in. She recalls that at the time, thrilled with her new popularity, she answered every letter personally. *Photoplay,* then the leading film publication under its influential editor-publisher James R. Quirk, ran her life story in installments and hailed her as a coming star in its reviews. Years later she said:

That fall of 1928 I went around with my little box camera taking pictures of every marquee that had my name in lights. From this period on, I was never again carefree. Before, I had been absolutely sure of myself in a brash and very young way. Now I began to study and observe myself. I was immersed with my own image on the screen (that will show you how immature I was). But I did have sense enough to know I must work, and work hard. I kept setting the goal higher and higher.

Her salary in 1925 had been $75 a week. By 1928 it was $500 a week.

Her 1929 films included another with Haines, *The Duke Steps Out*. She was a college student in love with a prizefighter (Haines) turned big-man-on-campus. Then she sang and danced in *Hollywood Revue of 1929*, a spectacular in which every MGM star except Garbo appeared.

Miss Crawford began to insist on stronger roles, to which Mayer, completely sold on her talent and future prospects, acceded. She co-starred with her husband, Douglas Fairbanks, Jr., in *Our Modern Maidens*, a sequel of sorts to her earlier *Dancing Daughters* hit. Once again she was, in the words of one critic, "the hard, ultra-modern, world-weary girl so prevalent in our contemporary life."

The talkies arrived full-force at this point, and Miss Crawford tackled them successfully. Her first sound appearance, in *Untamed*, brought kind words from the critics for her resonant and pleasant voice, which enhanced her screen image and reinforced her stardom. In this respect she proved luckier than Haines, John Gilbert, and many others whose popularity evaporated with sound. *Untamed* displayed her as a girl raised in the South American wilds who learns civilized manners the hard way when she finds herself an heiress transplanted to New York. Robert Montgomery, in his first co-starring stint with her, played the young man who furthered her re-education.

The 1930 Crawford then entered her "imitate Garbo" phase. Along with Tallulah Bankhead, Marlene Dietrich, and other enterprising sirens of the time, she offered her version of the Garbo hair-do, enigmatic expression, and remote, languorous manner. Her makeup underwent a profound change. Her eyes, always prominent and expressive, were accentuated, the hollows of her cheeks were shaded and her mouth was reshaped by a new lipstick approach—a wide, red smear across her lower face. This, along with her big eyes, would soon become a Crawford trademark.

Adrian, the famous MGM designer, then took over her clothes-image. Miss Crawford later wrote:

"Adrian had a profound effect both on my professional and personal life. He put the ruffles in the right places and showed me how to dress. Right timing is always important—a picture, a book, or a style can be too early or too late. Adrian's style timing has always been right. From 1929 to 1943 this creative, resourceful man designed everything I wore in pictures and most of what I wore in my personal life. The clothes he designed for MGM pictures had a very great impact, not only on the picture business but on the style of the whole country. In fact, I don't remember any 'fashions' before Adrian. My style had been bows—everywhere. Adrian toned me down, not in color but in line, and gave me the tailored look that was so distinctive.

"He decided to emphasize my broad, square shoulders, and this became an overnight sensation in the 1930s and dominated women's styles for more than ten years. Adrian, a true artist, always subdued for dramatic scenes. But for a lighter scene, he would create a 'big' dress."

Miss Crawford's films in 1930 were rather inconsequential, but they did increase her following. *Montana Moon* cast her as a wealthy rancher's daughter involved in an on-again-off-again romance with a cowboy. *Our Blushing Brides* was a cross between the three-girls-in-love-and-career clichés of *Sally, Irene and Mary* and the flashy, modern-girl doings of *Our Dancing Daughters*. But late in the year she did better with *Paid*, an adaptation of the celebrated Broadway play *Within the Law*. Miss Crawford played a girl unjustly sentenced to prison, who later seeks revenge.

By 1931, millions of young American women were identifying with Miss Crawford and imitating her clothes, walk, speech, and general appearance. *Dance Fools Dance* showcased her as a rich girl turned crime reporter when her family loses its money in the Crash. This was her first pairing with Clark Gable, who had a secondary role as a gangster. *Laughing Sinners* presented her as a fallen woman rescued by Gable, who played a Salvation Army officer. *This Modern Age* cast her as a society girl who gets into romantic misadventures in Paris.

Late 1931 brought her a glossy and well-mounted soap opera called *Possessed*. She and Gable won good reviews for it. (This was the first of two films she made under the same title but with different stories; the second *Possessed* was made for Warner's sixteen years later.) The MGM *Possessed* was about a fortune-hunter (Miss Crawford) who becomes the mistress of a rich and powerful New York attorney (Gable) who aspires to a political career. It was advertised as a film "for those who like their film fare hot and the morals of their screen heroines loose."

From 1932 on, her films were invested with a production polish and careful mounting that rivaled those accorded Greta Garbo and Norma Shearer. The latter star, as the wife of prestigious and gifted MGM producer Irving Thalberg, commanded quality vehicles. Miss Crawford's acting continued to improve; she showed up well in *Grand Hotel* as the ambitious, amoral stenographer Flaemmchen, holding her own with such expert performers as John and Lionel Barrymore and Wallace Beery. Her next film, *Letty Lynton*, displayed her as a wealthy playgirl torn between a South American rogue (Nils Asther) and a Manhattan society boy (Robert Montgomery).

She then made a crucial mistake: She took on the role in *Rain* that Jeanne Eagels had made famous on the stage. Sadie Thompson was a complex characterization that required the interpretation of a top-flight actress. Gloria Swanson had given a creditable account of herself in a 1928 silent version, and Joan Crawford felt that a success in this bravura role would enhance her prestige and solidify her gains. But at twenty-four, as she was publicly to admit years later, she was still too immature artistically to do the role sufficient justice. In retrospect, she feels that her performance lacked shading and discipline, and that she should have heeded director Lewis Milestone's ideas about the role. MGM loaned her out to United Artists for this film, which was a resounding failure with both critics and public.

At this time personal problems complicated Miss Crawford's life. She was plagued with a series of miscarriages, and finally her marriage to Douglas Fairbanks, Jr. collapsed. They were divorced in the spring of 1933.

She then fell in love with her co-star, Clark Gable, but felt that marriage was not in the cards for them. Gable was already married, and Miss Crawford said years later that she felt at the time that he desired only those women he couldn't have and lost interest in those who were too available.

Her first picture with the man who was to be her second husband, Franchot Tone, was *Today We Live*. Released in early 1933, it was a World War I aerial romance co-starring Gary Cooper. The film opened to lukewarm reviews.

She and Tone made other pictures together. She was greatly impressed with his theatrical background, his erudition, cultivated mind, and aristocratic manners. In October, 1935, they were married. She later said that she had learned a great deal from Tone, and to this day they are warm friends, though their marriage lasted only four years.

The downward trend of *Today We Live* was reversed with *Dancing Lady*, released in November, 1933. In it, she played the star of a Broadway musical. Gable was the stage manager and Tone her rich admirer. Once again she was permitted to put her dancing expertise to good use.

Miss Crawford's 1934 films, all popular at the box office, offered variations on her established pattern. In *Sadie McKee*, again with Tone, she was the poor-girl-on-the-make. In *Chained,* she was the apex of a conventional romantic triangle, consisting of lover Clark Gable and husband Otto Kruger. Another triangle romance, with Gable again plus Robert Montgomery, was *Forsaking All Others.*

By 1935, she was being dubbed a "clotheshorse de luxe." Her pictures were handsomely mounted, lavishly styled by Adrian, but the plots—and Miss Crawford's image—were increasingly wooden and remote. *No More Ladies* was another well-tooled but superficial society drama in which Miss Crawford, married to Robert Montgomery, sought to keep her philanderer husband guessing via a phony romance with Franchot Tone. In *I Live My Life* she was a New York society girl involved with a stuffy archaeologist, played expertly by Brian Aherne.

Her last box-office year was 1936. The public was tiring of her increasingly stereotyped roles, and the critics complained that she wasn't working hard enough at deepening her acting skills. In *The Gorgeous Hussy,* a lavish costume film, Miss Crawford was Peggy Eaton, the notorious innkeeper's daughter who, in the 1830s, became the scandal of President Andrew Jackson's administration, and rose through a series of gossiped-about romances to be-

With her first husband, Douglas Fairbanks, Jr., in 1930

With her second husband, Franchot Tone, around 1935

With her good friend writer-publicist Jerry Asher, about 1934. Mr. Asher died in July, 1967.

With her third husband, Phillip Terry, at the time of their marriage in 1942.

come the wife of a cabinet member. The period costumes and setting were spectacular and the direction of Clarence Brown was sure-handed, but the critics said she was too "modern" for historical roles and complained that she was "on the same old glamor wagon."

A late 1936 offering was *Love on the Run.* In this bit of fluff she was a mad-cap heiress on the lam from an unwanted marriage to a European nobleman. She gets involved with two reporters (Clark Gable and Franchot Tone) who help her escape, and the three wander across Europe undergoing assorted humorous adventures. The critics shrugged.

The year 1937 accelerated her now evident professional decline. *The Last of Mrs. Cheyney,* a rehash of a 1929 Norma Shearer film, cast her as a lacquered jewel thief making mischief in English country homes, and *The Bride Wore Red* was thin Cinderella stuff about an Italian cabaret girl masquerading as an heiress at a resort in the Tyrol. Tone and Robert Young co-starred.

Neither film did too well at the box office. In early 1938, a movie trade paper labeled her "box-office poison" along with some other stars; but Mayer's faith in her durability was unshaken and she was signed to a new five-year contract. She was then cast in *Mannequin* opposite Spencer Tracy. Once more she was a poor girl who marries a millionaire (Tracy) after suffering at the hands of a heel (Alan Curtis), but the film had the benefit of the production talents of Joseph L. Mankiewicz, who, along with director Frank Borzage, managed to give the picture some substance and depth.

Miss Crawford continued to shop on her own for properties she considered promising; she persuaded Mayer to buy a literate drama of marital infidelity that she had seen as a play in New York. *The Shining Hour,* a late-1938 release, co-starred Melvyn Douglas, Margaret Sullavan, and Robert Young, with Fay Bainter giving strong support, and Miss Crawford more than held her own among these talented players. The critics were not unkind, but the public response was tepid. Nor did her next film help the situation: *Ice Follies of 1939* was an uneasy hodgepodge about an ice skater (Miss Crawford) who becomes a movie star and her ice-follies-entrepreneur husband (James Stewart) who resents their career separations. The ice skaters hogged the scene, and critics and public were unimpressed.

Crawford at this point felt beleaguered. Her marriage to Franchot Tone, like her first, was plagued with miscarriages, and in 1939 it ended. With a generosity and humility she has often displayed, Miss Crawford later said that she felt Tone's abilities had been superior to her own, but the disparity in their respective careers—she was a star; he never rose above leading man status—had wounded his ego and proven the one flaw in their otherwise fulfilled relationship. With her longing for motherhood frustrated, her career declining,

her marriage in ashes, Miss Crawford summoned her usual resiliency and went after a meaty role—Crystal in *The Women,* the trenchant Clare Boothe play that MGM was about to bring to the screen.

She recalls: "I had been a flapper in the age of flappers, and a sophisticated lady in an era of sophistication, and at first I didn't realize how limiting this was. By 1939, I was impatient for different roles. I begged for the part of the heavy in *The Women.* Mr. Mayer was dubious. I pleaded with him, with producer Hunt Stromberg, finally with George Cukor, who was going to direct."

Her persistence eventually won the role for her, and it proved to be a major turning point. George Cukor, famed for his guidance of women stars, proved, according to Miss Crawford, to be "a hard taskmaster, a painstaking director, and he took me over the coals, made me rehearse over and over, not just lines but even words. He gave me the roughest time I ever had, and I'm eternally grateful."

Cukor made her concentrate on voice and projection, and Crawford the Craftswoman was impressively unveiled in *The Women.* The critics immediately took note of the new level she had reached and she more than held her own in the reviews against such talents as Norma Shearer, Rosalind Russell, and Mary Boland.

Her next picture, *Strange Cargo,* released in early 1940, reunited her with Clark Gable, then at his zenith after his triumph in *Gone With the Wind.* The role did not permit her much range or footage. In this, she was a cabaret singer who joins a group of convicts escaping from Devil's Island and falls in love with one of them (Gable).

She considered this picture a minor setback, and when Norma Shearer refused the film version of the sparkling Gertrude Lawrence play, *Susan and God,* Crawford begged for it, and got it. George Cukor again directed, disciplining and refining her into a fresh technique that showed in the completed footage. Seen today, this picture about a flighty society matron who neglects her husband and child for a religious cult while ignoring religion's true spirit, holds up very well; Miss Crawford is excellent in it, as is Fredric March, who plays her husband.

Determined to consolidate her gains, Miss Crawford asked Louis B. Mayer to purchase *A Woman's Face,* a heavy drama about a horribly scarred woman whose emotions become distorted. Ingrid Bergman had made it as a Swedish film. Again George Cukor guided her through a creditable performance, and critics and public regarded her with a new respect.

A Woman's Face, released in 1941, was Miss Crawford's high point at MGM. The picture had the benefit of careful atmosphere, subtle performances by Conrad Veidt, Melvyn Douglas, and Albert Bassermann, a lavish mounting, good writing and direction, and a meticulously detailed, solidly thought-out performance by the star herself.

But the pictures that followed it were somewhat of a letdown. The remake of *When Ladies Meet*, opposite Greer Garson and Robert Taylor, was well-mounted soap opera and it did nothing for Miss Crawford, though her performance maintained the standards she had attained under Cukor's guidance. In January, 1942, Carole Lombard was killed in a plane crash, and Miss Crawford, in a loan-out to Columbia, took on her scheduled role in *They All Kissed the Bride*. In this she played a stuffy, arrogant career woman who is deflated and mellowed by Melvyn Douglas. The film was a sophisticated comedy, and the critics implied that this sort of role was not her forte, that Lombard would have made more of the role.

Back at MGM she was in two bad films in a row. *Reunion in France* was shallow, tepid stuff about a fashion designer in the Paris of 1940 who falls in love with a Nazi collaborator (Philip Dorn), who later turns out to have been a patriot all along. John Wayne was on hand as an American pilot with whom she has a passing romance. One reviewer, after dismissing other aspects of the film, commented: "Despite reports of limited yardgoods and costume budgets in Hollywood (it was mid-World War II) Miss Crawford manages to appear in a new gown in virtually every scene."

The picture that followed, *Above Suspicion*, was no help to Miss Crawford's declining career fortunes. Fred MacMurray co-starred in some unbelievable fluff about a honeymooning couple in Nazi Germany who are actually spies for the British. Critics and public registered solid indifference. It was Miss Crawford's last MGM film for a decade.

She said later of this sterile period: "Mr. Mayer didn't want me to leave, but he knew how unhappy I was. I left by the back gate. I loved MGM—it was home. But I longed for challenging parts and I wasn't getting them. There were top executives who thought me all washed up. They still regarded me as Letty Lynton. They actually laughed when I wanted to do pictures like *Random Harvest* and *Madame Curie*. If you think I made poor films at MGM after *A Woman's Face*, you should have seen the ones I went on suspension *not* to make!"

At this low point, she married a retiring, gentlemanly young actor named Phillip Terry, who had been playing minor roles in films. Terry was cultured and bookish, but after three years Miss Crawford recognized that this marriage also had been a mistake. "I hadn't loved Phillip enough," she said later. "I married because I was unutterably lonely. Don't *ever* marry because of loneliness. I've owed him an apology from the first."

Soon after her divorce from Franchot Tone, Miss Crawford had adopted a baby girl, Christina. During her marriage to Terry she adopted a boy, Christopher. Later she took into her home twin girls, Cathy and Cynthia. All are now grown. What-

ever Miss Crawford's marital problems have been, she did concentrate, most creditably, on making the lives of her four adopted children good, and she fulfilled her maternal duties despite the pressures of a busy career.

For two years after leaving MGM she did not work. In 1943 she had signed a contract with Warner Brothers for a third of what MGM had paid her, but she could not find a script that satisfied her and asked to be taken off salary. "What does the woman want?" Jack Warner reportedly asked his executives. She relayed back the answer: "Good pictures!"

Miss Crawford credits Lew Wasserman, then an agent and later MCA president, with "keeping me going and giving me back my confidence in myself. Thanks to him I came to believe that I was *not* through."

The late producer Jerry Wald, then at Warners, found *Mildred Pierce*. As soon as Crawford read the script she knew it was right for her. It was a hard-boiled but literate and intelligent story of a woman who rises from waitress to restaurant tycoon, all the while loving, and overindulging, her spoiled young daughter. Miss Crawford's only 1944 appearance had been as one of a group of Warner Brothers stars in *Hollywood Canteen. Mildred Pierce* was not released until the fall of 1945. It proved well worth waiting for.

The role of Mildred had depth and dimension and under Michael Curtiz's direction Miss Crawford gave a technically expert and fully realized interpretation that won her the 1945 Academy Award and restored her to stardom. Later she said of Michael Curtiz: "He stripped off my Adrian shoulder pads and rubbed my makeup down to some hard-pan character."

Her next two Warner Brothers films maintained the standard of *Mildred Pierce. Humoresque*, released in late 1946, showcased her as the dissolute, wealthy patroness of an aspiring young violinist, played by John Garfield. Her professional confidence had been restored by the Oscar she had just won, and she moved through the role with great aplomb and self-assurance, radiating an authority and magnetism that were irresistible.

Then came a picture which many, including this writer and Miss Crawford herself, consider her high-water mark at Warners. In *Possessed*, released in mid-1947, she played an emotionally unstable woman who becomes the victim of her too intense emotions, sliding gradually into madness under the strain of an unrequited love. Van Heflin, as the object of her affections, gave her able support, and the cast, including Raymond Massey and Geraldine Brooks, offered fine performances under the polished direction of Curtis Bernhardt. For this, Miss Crawford was nominated for the 1947 Academy Award.

Daisy Kenyon, a late-1947 release, reverted unfortunately to the soap-opera clichés that had marred her mid-1930s MGM career. Loaned out to 20th Century-Fox for this film, Miss Crawford played a Greenwich Village commercial artist who couldn't make up her mind between a high-powered (and married) lawyer (Dana Andrews) and an ex-soldier of more modest pretensions who offers her a wedding ring (Henry Fonda).

Back at Warners in early 1948, Miss Crawford sensed fresh career trouble, and she spent most of the year hunting for a substantial role. One script that she felt had possibilities, *Flamingo Road*, was constructed more or less along *Mildred Pierce* lines. She asked that the script be rewritten, and finally went ahead with the picture. Again she was a woman of humble origins who climbs in the world on a ladder of men, including Zachary Scott and David Brian. The setting was a small Southern town. Miss Crawford runs afoul of the political boss (Sidney Greenstreet) and kills him at the end in a burst of melodrama. Michael Curtiz's direction and careful mounting failed to disguise the picture's essential flimsiness. Nor could anything kinder be said of her next film, *The Damned Don't Cry*, in which she was the rags-to-riches mistress of a crime-cartel boss, played by David Brian. She also made a brief appearance in a Dennis Morgan–Jack Carson 1949 release, *It's a Great Feeling*.

Again on the hunt for solid dramatic fare, Miss Crawford wangled a loan-out to Columbia for a re-make of *Craig's Wife*, a 1936 hit that had starred Rosalind Russell. Retitled *Harriet Craig* and ably directed by Vincent Sherman, it was a creditable effort; Miss Crawford gave an excellent account of herself as an unloving and tyrannical wife who subconsciously expresses her contempt for her husband (Wendell Corey) and all men by deifying her house and its appurtenances above her marriage and other human contacts.

At Warners in early 1951, Miss Crawford decided to risk *Goodbye, My Fancy*, which had been a Broadway play about a congresswoman who returns to her alma mater for an honorary degree. While there she resumes an old romance with the college president (Robert Young) and gets involved in matters of academic freedom. The political aspect which had given the play some substance was edited out, however, and Miss Crawford feels today that this omission took the guts out of the picture.

Her next for Warners was *This Woman Is Dangerous*, in which she was a racketeer's mistress (David Brian again) who falls in love with an eye surgeon (Dennis Morgan) who has operated on her for impending blindness. This picture was so far below the hard-won standards she had set for herself that she asked to be relieved of her Warner Brothers contract.

Again on her own, Miss Crawford began reading scripts and finally signed with independent producer Joseph Kaufman to do *Sudden Fear*. This turned out to be a well-mounted, tastefully directed (by David Miller) thriller about a rich playwright

Congratulated by director Michael Curtiz when she won the 1945 Academy Award for Mildred Pierce

(Miss Crawford) who discovers she is the target of a murder that is being plotted by her husband (Jack Palance) and his mistress (Gloria Grahame). In this she ran the gamut of emotions from dawning infatuation to tearful disenchantment to wild-eyed terror. Again she won an Academy Award nomination as the best actress of 1952.

MGM, to her great satisfaction, then asked her back for one picture, *Torch Song*. Released in 1953, in handsome Technicolor, it displayed Miss Crawford, then forty-five, as a temperamental musical-comedy star who falls in love with a blind pianist, played by Michael Wilding. In it she danced for the first time in many years. Her old friend William Haines, who has since become a well-known Hollywood interior decorator, came on the set to watch her rehearse the dance scenes, and laughingly told her, "Only God could get your legs that high!"

Torch Song demonstrated the efficacy of one of Miss Crawford's lifelong disciplines: the care of her body with diet, exercise, and proper living. Her figure was slim as ever, her appearance belied her years, and her dancing, under director Chuck Walters' able coaching, proved to be as lithe as it was in *Our Dancing Daughters*.

She now decided to vary her pace with a Western, her first since the Tim McCoy days. *Johnny Guitar*, for Republic, displayed her as the mistress of a saloon who creates dissension among the men vying for her favors. Sterling Hayden and Scott Brady co-starred. This one left the critics cold, and she

On a trip to Europe circa 1956 with her husband Alfred Steele and their children (left to right) Christopher, twins Cathy and Cynthia, and Christina.

next journeyed over to Universal for *Female on the Beach.* Though she tried to invest this potboiler with substance and vitality, the tale of a rich and lonely widow and a beach-bum, played by Jeff Chandler, emerged as stylish and occasionally engrossing but nonetheless soapy.

Miss Crawford then decided to accept an offer from Columbia Pictures for several films on a percentage-of-the-gross deal. *Queen Bee,* released late in 1955, revealed her as the oversexed, neurotic mistress of a Southern mansion who wreaks havoc on the men around her. The critics said she overacted and that the dramatics were cheap and synthetic. *Autumn Leaves,* her one 1956 effort, was better received. Though not one of her best pictures, it did have the benefit of painstaking direction by Robert Aldrich, and Miss Crawford's acting, despite the occasional melodramatics of the plot, was sincere and restrained. In this she was a lonely spinster who falls in love with and marries an emotionally tormented young man (Cliff Robertson) who becomes psychotic.

Her third for Columbia, released in late 1957, was *The Story of Esther Costello.* She played a rich American who visits her birthplace in Ireland, adopts a deaf-mute she meets there (winningly played by Heather Sears), and helps her to make a new life. Complications ensue when her amoral husband (Rossano Brazzi) rapes her helpless young charge. The picture drew good notices, with the critics praising her acting.

This was Miss Crawford's last picture for two years. In 1955, she had married Alfred Steele, Board Chairman of Pepsi-Cola, and in the years that followed she transferred her activities increasingly to New York. Soon she was heavily involved in the affairs of the famous soft drink company, and traveled a great deal with her husband on company business. After his death in 1959, she was named to Pepsi-Cola's board of directors and has been active with the company ever since. The acumen, drive, and intelligence she had brought to her Hollywood career have served her well in this new field. Miss Crawford is now considered one of the country's more successful businesswomen.

In 1959, Jerry Wald, then at 20th Century-Fox, offered her the role of Amanda Farrow in *The Best of Everything,* the film version of the Rona Jaffe novel about the love lives of career women in the publishing field. Alfred Steele had just died, and she took the rather brief part in order to get her mind off her sorrow. She played an editor, in love with a married man, whose waspish temperament makes her the terror of the office. Some critics commented that she was the only solid thing in the picture and that she gave it "class."

Miss Crawford was off the screen for another three years. Then, in 1962, she co-starred, again on a percentage-of-the-gross deal, with Bette Davis in *What Ever Happened to Baby Jane?* This turned out

With director Robert Aldrich and Bette Davis just before the Davis-Crawford co-starrer What Ever Happened to Baby Jane? *opened in 1962*

to be one of the biggest hits of the year, and a box-office winner to boot. The macabre tale of two aging sisters, former movie stars, and the hatred and mutual suspicion that distorts their life together, brought more attention to Bette Davis than to Miss Crawford, who had the more passive role, but it reinforced the careers of both stars, who then found themselves in a "horror film" cycle for some years.

In 1963, Miss Crawford had a brief role as a tyrannical head nurse with out-of-date ideas in a drama about mental hospital conditions, *The Caretakers*. In 1964, she starred for William Castle in another "horror" film, *Strait Jacket*. This was a Columbia Pictures release about an axe murderess who is released from a hospital for the criminally insane and is suspected of a fresh homicidal binge. Most critics thought it cheap-jack, unworthy of her talents.

In 1964, she arranged to co-star again with Bette Davis in 20th Century-Fox's *Hush, Hush, Sweet Charlotte*, but an attack of pneumonia forced her withdrawal from the picture. After recuperating, Miss Crawford did a small role in a Universal "horror" film called *I Saw What You Did*. She played a sexually frustrated woman who is in love with a handsome neighbor (John Ireland) who turns out to be a murderer. Despite her peripheral role (the action centered about two teen-age girls who accidentally expose the murderer), Miss Crawford got top billing. The critics were lukewarm toward both picture and cast.

Since 1965, she has done only one film, *Berserk*, but is currently contracting to do others. *Berserk*, a 1968 release for Columbia and her eightieth film, showcases her as the manager of an English circus who is suspected of a series of murders. Critics continue to hope that Miss Crawford will escape the "horror film" cycle which box-office considerations seem to have forced on her of late, and that she will land a vehicle worthy of the seasoned expertise she has developed in the picture medium over four hard-working decades.

Meanwhile her career with Pepsi-Cola keeps Miss Crawford busy and happy. She delights in the progress of her grown children, and maintains her usual disciplined business and social schedule. She has made a number of creditable appearances in television dramas over the years, and is a sought-after guest on panel and celebrity shows.

Certainly she has aged gracefully and has kept up her vital interest in the world around her. She continues to live by such long-held personal codes as "Frustrations are to work through, and even if you fail, the trying enriches you" and "Turn pressure into a challenge and enjoy it."

Doubtless it is the optimistic, courageous philosophy that these codes imply that has made her at age sixty one of the most respected women in both film and business circles.

ss Crawford at the time she made The Caretakers *(1963)*

The Films of
Joan Crawford

Pretty Ladies

A Metro-Goldwyn-Mayer Picture
(1925)

CAST: ZaSu Pitts, Tom Moore, Ann Pennington, Lilyan Tashman, Bernard Randall, Helen D'Algy, Conrad Nagel, Norma Shearer, George K. Arthur, Lucille LeSueur [Joan Crawford], Paul Ellis, Roy D'Arcy, Gwendolyn Lee, Dorothy Seastrom, Lew Harvey, Chad Huber, Walter Shumway, Dan Crimmins, Jimmy Quinn.

CREDITS: From the story by Adela Rogers St. Johns. Adapted by Alice D. G. Miller. Directed by Monta Bell. Cameraman, Ira H. Morgan. Running time, 74 minutes.

SYNOPSIS

The film is a re-creation of the Ziegfeld Follies, with fictional characters interwoven with thinly disguised take-offs on famed personalities, including Flo Ziegfeld, Eddie Cantor, Will Rogers, and Gallagher and Shean. Ann Pennington, famed Follies star, appears as herself. Joan Crawford, in this, her first film, has a small role as Bobby, one of the showgirls. (She was billed for the first and only time as Lucille LeSueur.) The plot is a simple one, interspersed with authentic glimpses of backstage Follies life and many interesting acts and production numbers, some in color. The Adela Rogers St. Johns story deals with Maggie Keenan (ZaSu Pitts) a dancing comedienne who is liked by everyone but loved by none. Regarded by the troupe as a physically unattractive but lovable and amusing clown, Maggie spends her off-stage hours in loneliness while the beautiful chorus girls date exciting men. In her solitude, Maggie has constructed a fantasy world starring a Dream Lover (played by Conrad Nagel), but despite this escapist consolation, she longs for a real-life, flesh-and-blood man. He appears finally in the person of a drummer, Al Cassidy (Tom Moore) who writes songs on the side. Al develops a sympathetic friendship for Maggie which falls short of love, while Maggie falls head over heels in love with him. Al writes a song with Maggie in mind, and it proves to be the hit of the show. He comes to love Maggie without being *in* love with her, and they marry. Maggie knows that her hold on Al is tenuous, but she is endlessly loving, long-suffering, and forgiving of his lapses. Al falls into the clutches of a scheming soubrette, Selma Larson (Lilyan Tashman), who seeks to use his talents to further her stage career. Al is unfaithful to the devoted Maggie and has a temporary affair with Selma. This breaks Maggie's heart. But soon Al comes to realize the truth about Selma; he returns to Maggie and asks her forgiveness. Maggie, who has demonstrated from the beginning the rare quality of loving with utter selflessness, takes him back with a glad heart and without recriminations.

Joan Crawford

What the critics said about PRETTY LADIES

"Sisk" in Variety

An expensive film devoted primarily to plugging the *Follies*, for it mentions that show by name several times. However, the thing of interest is that a very reliable actress, ZaSu Pitts, gets her first really big chance and comes through like a million dollars. The fault with the film is that either (Monta) Bell or the producers have tried to mix a spectacle of New York's theatrical world with an absorbing human interest story. Most of the revue scenes are shown in color. Living chandeliers and undressed ladies, usual revue adjuncts, are to be seen.

In the New York Times

Here is one of those back-stage photoplays, with a very commonplace story, and yet it has been made a thoroughly worthwhile film. The external evidence is all to the effect that the directing is what made it. Monta Bell is the director. He deserves the highest praise for this piece of work turned out of his studio.

In the New York American

If the footlights hold a glamour for you, don't stay away from this picture. *Pretty Ladies* starts off with a rattling good story by Adela Rogers St. Johns. It's not just a hoked-up plot to keep some high-salaried actress at work. The plot is simple but dramatic. And Alice D. G. Miller has adapted it splendidly. The cast is much too long and too good to describe in detail, but ZaSu Pitts, Tom Moore and Lilyan Tashman deserve special praise.

With unidentified player and Tom Moore

With ZaSu Pitts

Old Clothes

A Metro-Goldwyn-Mayer Picture

(1925)

CAST: Jackie Coogan, Joan Crawford, Max Davidson, Lillian Elliott, Alan Forrest, James Mason, Stanton Heck.

CREDITS: From the story by Willard Mack. Produced by Jack Coogan, Sr. Directed by Eddie Cline. Cameraman, Frank B. Good. Running time, 65 minutes.

SYNOPSIS

Timothy Kelly (Jackie Coogan) and Max Ginsburg (Max Davidson) are partners in the old clothes and junk business. Timothy, young as he is, is the hard-headed, practical partner, while Max is the lovable loser with unwise business judgment. One of the reasons for their straitened circumstances is an unwise investment they have made in a certain stock, Vista Copper. One of their upstairs bedrooms is papered with Vista stock. Timothy has befriended a destitute young girl, Mary Riley (Joan Crawford), and he and Max take her into their home as a boarder. Timothy gets Mary a job in the office of a rich young Wall Streeter, Nathan Burke (Alan Forrest) and Nathan and Mary fall in love. But Nathan's mother (Lillian Elliott) is a snob and feels Mary is an unsuitable alliance for her son. However, Mary and Nathan continue to see each other secretly, aided and abetted by the practical but sympathetic Timothy and the impractical but amiable Max. Mary and Timothy become close friends, and tell each other all their troubles. Meanwhile, things are not going so well for young Wall Streeter Nathan, who has made unwise stock maneuvers. One night he comes to see Mary, Timothy, and Max and tells them that if he could only corner a certain stock, a crucial element in his current financial manipulations, his fortunes would go sky-high. Otherwise he faces disaster. Of course, the name of the specific stock comes up in the conversation: Vista. Timothy takes Nathan upstairs to show him the room wall-papered with the precious stock, and all ends happily, with Nathan and Mary overcoming his mother's disapproval and marrying, and Timothy and Max back on Easy Street.

What the critics said about OLD CLOTHES

Louella O. Parsons in the New York Journal-American

The girl, Joan Crawford, is a discovery of Jack Coogan, Sr. She is very attractive, and shows promise.

Delight Evans in the New York Morning Telegraph

The love interest, supplied by Alan Forrest and Joan Crawford, should satisfy such spectators as the antics of the small star fail to amuse—if any.

In Variety

Little Coogan wears a big derby hat, walks with his hands behind his back, and is generally grown up. The others fulfill their roles satisfactorily, and to the credit of Eddie Cline, the director, it must be said that he has injected clever business at spots. Inasmuch as the recent Coogan films haven't done so well, and as this one is cheaply produced, it doesn't seem to be in the stars that *Old Clothes* will be a mop-up for anybody.

With Jackie Coogan

With Jackie Coogan

The Only Thing

A Metro-Goldwyn-Mayer Picture

(1925)

CAST: Eleanor Boardman, Conrad Nagel, Edward Connelly, Arthur Edmond Carew, Louis Payne, Vera Lewis, Carrie Clarke Ward, Constance Wylie, Dale Fuller, Ned Sparks, David Mir, Mario Carillo, Michael Pleschkoff, Buddy Smith, Joan Crawford, Frank Braidwood, Derke Glynne, Mary Hawes.

CREDITS: From the novel by Elinor Glyn. Story by Elinor Glyn and picture made under Miss Glyn's personal supervision. Directed by Jack Conway. Cameraman, Chester Lyons. Running time, 62 minutes.

SYNOPSIS

Thyra, Princess of Svendborg (Eleanor Boardman) is affianced to the King of Chekia (Edward Connelly), a repulsive, aging roué. When she arrives at the Court of Chekia, Thyra is appalled at the King's unattractive appearance and manners, but determines to do her duty by her native land and sacrifice herself to him for reasons of state.

Chekia, badly governed and burdened with a corrupt aristocracy, is approaching social chaos, and a revolution is imminent. The Duke of Chevenix (Conrad Nagel), representing the King of England, arrives at court for the marriage. He and Princess Thyra meet and fall in love. The Duke is appalled at the idea of her marrying the King, and determines to woo her away from him. But despite her love for the Duke, the Princess is determined to do her duty. The court in which Thyra finds herself is a veritable grotesquerie, with corrupt nobles and ugly princesses, all unwed sisters of the equally ugly king. On the night before the wedding, the Duke enters the Princess's chamber and begs her to flee with him, but she continues to maintain that her country's interests come first. That same night, the long-expected revolution erupts, led by the fiery Gigberto (Arthur Edmond Carew). The King is assassinated during the rioting, and all aristocrats are arrested and led before the Revolutionary Tribunal. Meanwhile, Gigberto has also fallen in love with the Princess, to the point where he stands ready to betray his cause for her love. Accordingly, the Revolutionists arrest their own leader, and an-

During the revolution

nounce that they will bind him and the Princess together and send them out to drown in a leaky barge. But the night before this watery double execution is to be expedited, the Duke changes places with Gigberto in his cell, and the Duke and Princess are sent out the next morning in the leaky barge. But true lovers are never allowed to perish in Elinor Glyn's Graustarkian romances, and they are rescued at the last minute from the barge by the Princess's home navy, the worthy men of a Svendborgian battleship. Joan Crawford had a tiny supporting role in this film, that of Young Lady Catherine, a member of the Court entourage.

What the critics said about THE ONLY THING

Regina Cannon in the New York Evening Graphic

Elinor Glyn's latest comic opera is a nightmare. It must have been inspired by a midnight reading of *Dante's Inferno, Three Weeks, Graustark* and *Scaramouche*. It was written, titled, supervised, and super-directed by the Madame herself. You know the answer. Of course it deals with kings, princesses, and dukes, yachts, palaces and revolutions—anything less than royalty Miss Glyn

would consider a waste of time. . . . We'd like to tell you what the story is all about, but we only saw the picture through once. We may know more later, because we're sending a complimentary ticket to a girl against whom we have a grudge.

In the New York Daily Mirror

The story duplicates the usual Elinor Glyn romance, only it lacks the novelty of her previous effusions.

In Variety

In directing, Conway did not particularly distinguish himself, but it is easy to assume that he may have been working under a handicap.

Norbert Lusk in the New York Morning Telegraph

[The picture] is entertaining from start to finish. Its pomp and splendor will please those who are easily pleased; its deft touches of characterization, its cynical subtitles and excellent acting will challenge the more critical. If the new picture lacks the sweep and intensity of Mrs. Glyn's *His Hour*, as some spectators undoubtedly will agree, it must be remembered that a different cast is seen in this and the locale is different.

Dancing with unidentified player

Sally, Irene and Mary

A Metro-Goldwyn-Mayer Picture
(1925)

CAST: Constance Bennett, Joan Crawford, Sally O'Neil, William Haines, Douglas Gilmore, Ray Howard, Aggie Herrin, Kate Price, Lillian Elliott, Henry Kolker, Sam DeGrasse, Mae Cooper.

CREDITS: From the musical play by Eddie Dowling and Cyrus Woods. Adapted by Edmund Goulding. Directed by Edmund Goulding. Cameraman, John Arnold. Running time, 58 minutes.

SYNOPSIS

Sally (Constance Bennett), Irene (Joan Crawford), and Mary (Sally O'Neil) are showgirls in a Broadway revue. All three have diametrically opposite approaches to life, love, and their careers. Sally is an ambitious, self-centered young lady, sure of her looks, charm, and ability, and ambitious to win a rich "sugar daddy." Well-heeled, if slightly superannuated, Marcus Morton (Henry Kolker) fills the bill. Irene is a sentimental, in-love-with-love type. She takes up with one of Broadway's champion cads and lady-killers, Glen Nester (Douglas Gilmore), while being assiduously if forlornly courted by a more sincere type, Charles Greenwood (Ray Howard). Mary is a perky little Irish girl from the tenements who is loved by a poor-but-honest young plumber, Jimmy Dungan (William Haines). But Mary is spunky and adventurous and wants to tear a leaf out of Sally's book. So she sets her cap for Sally's millionaire. The backstage life of the typical revue girl, circa 1925, is detailed. For every one who is wined and dined on lobster and champagne in exclusive night clubs, ten go home to corned beef and cabbage and the problems of ripped stockings and making-do-till-payday. With the exception of the sentimental, unrealistic Irene, the girls eventually land on their feet. Sally finally achieves an enduring relationship with her sugar-daddy and Mary, disenchanted in time with her pursuit of the high life, goes back to Jimmy the Plumber. Irene's end is tragic. She has fallen in love with Glen, who is a trifler and a chronic womanizer and seeks only a sex experience with her. She goes to his apartment, where he tries to seduce her. Irene for all her dreaminess, is basically a good girl with firm moral standards, and she resists him, hoping that in time he will marry her. But Glen tells her that she has never meant more than an affair to him, and since she won't cooperate, she can get out. Irene leaves Glen's apartment in tears, meets her long-suffering suitor, and in a state of frenzied, rebound-type hysteria, agrees to run away with him and be married. While she and Charles are racing a train to a crossing, they are killed in a collision with the train.

With Henry Kolker

With Constance Bennett and Sally O'Neil

What the critics said about
SALLY, IRENE AND MARY

In the New York World

Sally, Irene and Mary, the eternal showgirls, the darlings of the musical comedy stage, have gone most successfully into the movies. From a sketchy plot, Edmund Goulding has wrought a picture amusing, light, so well done that it is a pity the contents mean so little. Without any call for histrionics, Constance Bennett, Joan Crawford, and Sally O'Neil in the title roles played with a polish to their performances that usually takes more years of experience to acquire than any of the three possess.

Regina Cannon in the New York Evening Graphic

[The film] is pretty cheap, tawdry, sentimental stuff poorly directed. The subtle touches (?) are put on with a shovel. But anyone who likes to see backstage life as it is sometimes lived may find some amusement in watching this tale unfold. Constance Bennett makes an alluring Sally and does the best work in the picture. Joan Crawford is a lovely Irene and Sally O'Neil as Mary is a pert youngster who is busy overacting every minute.

James R. Quirk in Photoplay

One of the nicest pictures of backstage chorus girl life that it has been our lot to see. For a change, we see the tinseled creatures as they really are—hard-working, ambitious youngsters who go home to corned beef and cabbage, usually, instead of to night clubs and broiled lobster. The picture as a whole is very well cast, the title roles perfectly so . . . Joan Crawford, as Irene, the sentimental one, gives a good performance. . . .

The Boob

A Metro-Goldwyn-Mayer Picture

(1926)

CAST: Gertrude Olmstead, George K. Arthur, Joan Crawford, Charles Murray, Antonio D'Algy, Hank Mann, Babe London.

CREDITS: Adapted by Kenneth Clarke from the story by George Scarborough and Annette Westbay. Directed by William A. Wellman. Titles by Katherine Hiliker and H. H. Caldwell. Cameraman, William Daniels. Running time, 64 minutes.

SYNOPSIS

Peter (George K. Arthur), an idealistic farm youth, lives in a world of romantic unrealities, and yearns for the nobler, simpler days when knights in armor rescued damsels in distress. Pete's best friend, Cactus Jim (Charles Murray), listens sympathetically to his dreams but is himself an escapist, of the bottle-swigging kind. Peter is in love with May (Gertrude Olmstead), who tends to regard him as a weakling and ne'er-do-well. May imagines herself in love with a smooth-talking young man from the city, Harry (Antonio D'Algy). Peter is jealous and, moreover, suspicious of the sleek Harry's background. He decides to check up on him, and comes to suspect that Harry is a rumrunner involved in illegal doings in the Wyoming town near Peter's farm. Peter, who has done everything he can to impress May, all the way from affecting outlandish cowboy outfits to writing poetry, decides that the best and most concrete way to win her respect is to join up with the prohibition agents, including

Jane (Joan Crawford.) Peter and the agents obtain incontrovertible proof that Harry is a rum-runner when they watch him dig up a coffin that contains a large stock of booze. Harry tries to escape the pursuing agents, and Peter jumps him in a speeding car. The car crashes, and Peter comes to in a strange room. Around his bed are May, her father, Jane, and Harry. The police come and arrest Harry, and a federal agent tells Peter, "You're a better man than any three of our staff." May is at last impressed with Peter and tells him she loves him.

What the critics said about THE BOOB

In the Baltimore Sun

A piece of junk. . . . The company has simply covered itself with water and become soaking wet, for this tale of a half-dumb boy who turned prohibition agent to convince his girl he had nerve is as wishy-washy as any pail of dishwater.

In the Film Daily

The development is of such an episodic nature, however, that the initial idea is eventually lost in a variety of comedy gags, slapstick and otherwise. . . .

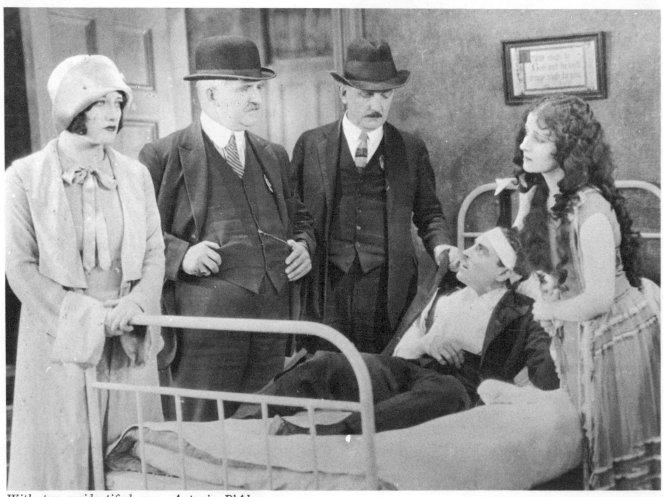

*With two unidentified men, Antonio D'Algy,
Gertrude Olmstead*

Tramp, Tramp, Tramp

A First National Picture

(1926)

CAST: Harry Langdon, Joan Crawford, Edwards Davis, Carlton Griffith, Alec B. Francis, Brooks Benedict, Tom Murray.

CREDITS: Story by Frank Capra, Tim Whelan, Hal Conklin, J. Frank Holliday, Gerald Duffy, and Murray Roth. Produced by Harry Langdon Corp. Directed by Harry Edwards. Cameramen, Elgin Lessley and George Spear. Running time, 62 minutes.

SYNOPSIS

Harry (Harry Langdon) is a ne'er-do-well who falls in love with a nice girl, Betty (Joan Crawford). Betty becomes his inspiration. Harry wants to better his lot so he can marry his girl, so he enters a cross-country hiking contest which will award $25,000 to the winner. He also plans to use part of this money to pay off the mortgage on the property of his father, Amos (Alec B. Francis). During the cross-country walking tournament, Harry gets into some outlandish and highly amusing situations, none of which faze his will to win. At one point, a flock of sheep ease him to a fence. He climbs over the fence, only to find himself on the edge of a steep precipice. At another point, Harry is arrested for stealing fruit and lands on a prison rock-pile, where he adopts ingenious methods to rid himself of the ball-and-chain. Later he gets caught in a cyclone, and weathers numerous other vicissitudes before finally trudging home the victor. Harry pays off his dad's mortgage, he and Betty get married, and the final sequence finds him essaying the role of "Young Harry" in a crib!

What one critic said about TRAMP, TRAMP, TRAMP

"Sisk" in Variety

Harry Langdon's first feature-length comedy. Langdon does some remarkable work. . . . Aside from the expert handling of all the gags assigned him, he does several long scenes in which facial expression is the only acting. Joan Crawford is borrowed from Metro to be a nice leading lady with little to do.

Paris

A Metro-Goldwyn-Mayer Picture

(1926)

CAST: Charles Ray, Joan Crawford, Douglas Gilmore, Michael Visaroff, Rose Dione, Jean Galeron.
CREDITS: Story by Edmund Goulding. Directed by Edmund Goulding. Cameraman, John Arnold. Running time, 67 minutes.

SYNOPSIS

Jerry (Charles Ray) is a carefree young American millionaire visiting in Paris. He has heard much of the apache way of life, and decides to investigate. In an apache den Jerry meets The Girl (Joan Crawford), makes up to her, and runs afoul of The Girl's boyfriend, The Cat (Douglas Gilmore), who knifes him. The Girl takes the wounded Jerry to her room and nurses him. She also tries to shield The Cat from the police, who come looking for him. Finally, The Girl persuades The Cat to go to prison so that later they can make a life together free from the threat of the law. Jerry wants to improve The Girl's lot; he has also fallen in love with her. He helps her with clothes and money and then offers to marry her, but she refuses him with the words, "You can't buy love." Theirs is strictly a platonic relationship, though there is a mutual friendship feeling, of a kind. Meanwhile The Girl thinks constantly of her loved one, The Cat. The Girl moves into Jerry's apartment and he lavishes luxuries on her. The Cat is released from prison, hears that The Girl is living with Jerry, and puts the wrong construction on their association. The Girl gets a note from The Cat and goes to rejoin him, and he attempts to choke her to death. A worried Jerry, following close behind, breaks in on them just in time to save her life. Jerry and The Cat struggle over the body of the unconscious girl, and Jerry is gradually choking the life out of The Cat when The Girl regains consciousness and begs him to desist. "I love him," she cries. The Girl and The Cat are reunited and Jerry goes sadly away.

What the critics said about PARIS

In Photoplay

If you leave before the final reel, you will find this an absorbing tale of love. Edmund Goulding, who wrote and directed it, slipped badly when he refused the happy ending. The girl, exquisitely played by Joan Crawford, should have married the young man about Paris night life, whom Charles Ray makes amusing and believable. Instead, she remains faithful to her sadistic apache, Douglas Gilmore. Good, but not to the last shot.

"Skig" in Variety

Strictly a "movie" idea of Paris, its apaches, and what can happen to a wealthy American youth in that environment. The objective is light comedy, occasionally reached, but it's all a bit silly. Advance information on Miss Crawford among the "picture mob" had her strongly heralded as a "comer." Undoubtedly a "looker" (when profiled she can double for Norma Shearer in a closeup), Miss Crawford will nevertheless have to show more talent than in this instance to make that billing entirely unanimous. Good, yes, but perhaps suffering from the pre-billing that always handicaps. And the . . . audience apparently got no decided impression.

Dancing with Douglas Gilmore

With Douglas Gilmore

The Taxi Dancer

A Metro-Goldwyn-Mayer Picture

(1927)

CAST: Joan Crawford, Owen Moore, Douglas Gilmore, Marc McDermott, William Orlamond, Gertrude Astor, Rockcliffe Fellowes, Claire McDowell, Bert Roach.

CREDITS: Story by Robert Terry Shannon. Adapted by A. P. Younger. Directed by Harry Millarde. Cameraman, Ira H. Morgan. Running time, 64 minutes.

SYNOPSIS

Joselyn Poe (Joan Crawford) a Virginia belle, decides to try her luck in New York. She has dancing talent, but she applies at a number of theatrical agencies without results. Downhearted after fruitless weeks at casting offices, she returns every evening to her furnished room in the West Forties and weeps on her bed. She is overheard by a neighbor, Lee Rogers (Owen Moore.) A cardshark by avocation, Lee has nonetheless an honest heart and noble instincts. Soon he's Joselyn's biggest morale-booster. Thanks to his interest and help she lands a job as a taxi dancer in a dime-a-dance emporium. Here Joselyn meets Kitty (Gertrude Astor), a Broadway chorus girl who dazzles Joselyn with tales of high life and Park Avenue parties. Soon Kitty has introduced Joselyn to a number of wealthy, unscrupulous men who prey on naïve girls. At one of the parties Joselyn meets Jim Kelvin (Douglas Gilmore), a goodlooking but shifty ballroom dancer. Joselyn falls blindly in love with him. Joselyn also encounters Henry Brierhalter (Marc McDermott), a lecherous millionaire with political connections. Joselyn's life revolves more and more about high-life parties, and back in the West Forties, Lee, who is wiser in the ways of the world, worries about her, realizes he is falling in love, and decides to go straight. "Broadway" Bates (Rockcliffe Fellowes), one of the Big Town's racier characters, is one of Joselyn's party hosts, and one night Bates is killed in a fight with Jim Kelvin. Joselyn tries to shield Jim from the police, and offers herself to Brierhalter in exchange for his political influence in Jim's behalf. But then Joselyn becomes disenchanted with Jim, and when she sees him in all his shoddiness and weakness, she comes to realize that the ever-faithful Lee is the real man of her heart. Lee and Joselyn return to her native Virginia, where presumably they settle down to a straight, simple, and happy life.

What the critics said about THE TAXI DANCER

James R. Quirk in Photoplay

Joan Crawford . . . rides high over the inferior material. Here is a girl of singular beauty and promise. And she certainly has IT. Just now she is very much in need of good direction.

"Sid" in Variety

Just another Southern girl come north to be pursued by men, but not unentertainingly. If anyone peeks too hard they'll find plenty of hoke. . . . Miss Crawford could be termed as an in and outer in this picture. Every so often comes a flash of power that may indicate this girl has something, while at other times she's too coy and clinging. That may be direction, too, albeit Millarde has handled both script and players well. There isn't much waste footage at any point. . . . *The Taxi Dancer* is one of those pictures that will do well in one town and flop in another. The flaps and their undergraduate or counter monarchs will remain interested, while older men won't find it hard to gaze on Miss Crawford and her array of nightgowns.

With Douglas Gilmore

Winners of the Wilderness

A Metro-Goldwyn-Mayer Picture

(1927)

CAST: Tim McCoy, Joan Crawford, Edward Connelly, Frank Currier, Roy D'Arcy, Louise Lorraine, Edward Hearn, Will R. Walling, Tom O'Brien, Chief Big Tree, Lionel Belmore.

CREDITS: Story by John Thomas Neville. Directed by W. S. Van Dyke. Cameraman, Clyde De Vinna. Running time, 68 minutes.

SYNOPSIS

Colonel O'Hara (Tim McCoy) is an intrepid army officer engaged in the fiercest fighting of the French and Indian wars of the mid-eighteenth century. He forms a romantic attachment to René Contrecoeur (Joan Crawford), daughter of General Contrecoeur (Edward Connelly), commander of the French forces. O'Hara, a dashing soldier of fortune, stalwart, honest, and brave, and an admirable wilderness fighter, is feared by both the French and the Indians, who constitute an increasing menace to the white men under their leader, Pontiac (Chief Big Tree). René and O'Hara are now deeply in love with each other, but must contend with the opposition of their respective associates, her family, and the exigencies of an uncertain war. Despairingly, they come to feel that the marriage they so long for will be indefinitely postponed. O'Hara, sent out to fight the Indians, is away for months. During this time René is captured by Pontiac's men. O'Hara and his troops track down the Indians who have spirited René away, a battle ensues, and she is rescued. During the course of his career, O'Hara wins the respect and commmendation of such assorted personages as General Washington (Edward Hearn), General Braddock (Will R. Walling), and Governor Dinwiddie (Lionel Belmore). But he also finds himself contending with the machinations of the villainous Captain Dumas (Roy D'Arcy), O'Hara's sworn enemy. Eventually, after O'Hara has won a number of military engagements and he is a hero, he and René finally find their way to a mutual happiness.

What one critic said about
WINNERS OF THE WILDERNESS

In Film Daily

Colonel Tim McCoy, a handsome soldier and a fine actor, mostly because he doesn't act. He is natural at all times. Joan Crawford the lady sought and Roy D'Arcy up to his usual deviltry.

With Tim McCoy

With Indians (unidentified players)

With unidentified player

With Francis X. Bushman, Jr.

The Understanding Heart

A Metro-Goldwyn-Mayer Picture

(1927)

CAST: Joan Crawford, Francis X. Bushman, Jr., Rockcliffe Fellowes, Carmel Myers, Richard Carle, Harry Clark.

CREDITS: From the story by Peter B. Kyne. Adapted by Edward T. Lowe, Jr. Directed by Jack Conway. Running time, 67 minutes.

SYNOPSIS

Monica Dale (Joan Crawford) is an observer for the Forest Rangers. She dwells high in the hills, and keeps a lookout for telltale wisps of smoke that presage dangerous forest flames. Monica is in love with stalwart ranger Tony Garland (Francis X. Bushman, Jr.). Bob Mason (Rockcliffe Fellowes) has run afoul of Monica's irresponsible and romantically frivolous sister-in-law, Kelcy Dale (Carmel Myers), and when Bob slays Kelcy's paramour in self-defense Kelcy hides her lover's gun; since there is no concrete proof of Bob's innocence, he is sent to prison. Subsequently, he escapes and takes refuge in Monica's forest observatory. Gradually Bob falls in love with Monica, whose heart continues to belong to Tony. Suddenly a major forest fire breaks out, and the observatory is surrounded by gradually encroaching rings of fire. Desperate methods of escape are being planned by Monica and Bob when a merciful rain quenches the flames. At the same time, parachutes are dropped by circling planes. The emergent triangle between Monica, Tony, and Bob is finally resolved when Bob demonstrates an "understanding heart" and relinquishes Monica to Tony after being cleared of the murder charge.

What the critics said about
THE UNDERSTANDING HEART

Betty Colfax in the New York Evening Graphic

Besides displaying no little ability as an actress, Miss Crawford screens remarkably well and shows a development so far beyond her work [in *The Taxi Dancer*] that one may expect important tidings of this young player.

In the Morning Telegraph

Joan Crawford has the most to do, and this gives her an edge on the other players.

The Unknown

A Metro-Goldwyn-Mayer Picture

(1927)

CAST: Lon Chaney, Joan Crawford, Norman Kerry, Nick de Ruiz, John George, Frank Lanning.

CREDITS: Story by Tod Browning. Scenario by Waldemar Young. Directed by Tod Browning. Cameraman, Merritt Gerstad. Running time, 65 minutes.

SYNOPSIS

Alonzo (Lon Chaney) is the armless wonder of the Zanzi Circus in Madrid. He can make his feet do the work of his hands, and he is the star of a sensational knife-throwing act in which—with his well-trained feet—he rings the figure of his beautiful young assistant, Estrellita (Joan Crawford), with lethal knives. Alonzo is desperately in love with Estrellita, who has a deep-rooted fear of men's arms and hands, which to her are symbols of encroaching sensual desire. Alonzo actually has normal arms, which he keeps strapped closely to his sides. He also has a deformity—a double thumb. These facts are known only to his assistant, Cojo (John George). Estrellita's father, Zanzi (Nick de Ruiz), is the circus manager. One night he physically abuses Alonzo, and in a fit of anger Alonzo frees his arms and murders Zanzi. The sole observer, Estrellita, had seen only a flash—of a double thumb. The police investigating the murder overlook Alonzo because they think he is armless. Though upset over having killed the father of the girl he loves, Alonzo continues his odd courtship, and Estrellita becomes fond of him—precisely, as Cojo warns Alonzo, because she thinks him armless. When Cojo adds that Estrellita may reject him when she learns he actually does have arms, the love-maddened Alonzo goes to a hospital and has them amputated. But when he returns to the circus after a lengthy recovery, he learns that the circus strong man, Malabar (Norman Kerry), has cured Estrellita of her fetish with his tender love and care, and that they will marry. In rage and despair, Alonzo tries to kill Malabar during a circus act by cutting the treadmill on which Malabar had placed two horses he is driving in opposite directions. But Estrellita, at considerable risk to her own life, quiets the horses, thus preventing the success of Alonzo's scheme, and Alonzo slips and is trampled to death by the horses.

What one critic said about THE UNKNOWN

Langdon W. Post in the New York Evening World

When Lon Chaney is in a picture, one can rest assured that that picture is worth seeing. When Joan Crawford and Norman Kerry are also present to help Mr. Chaney put it over, its value is that much enhanced. Not only is Mr. Chaney a very remarkable actor, but he almost invariably chooses a good story with which to display his talents, a practice all too seldom indulged in, in the case of other stars of his prominence. Joan Crawford is one of the screen's acknowledged artists and each picture seems to merely justify this characterization. Certainly her performance in this picture is a most impressive one.

Twelve Miles Out
A Metro-Goldwyn-Mayer Picture
(1927)

CAST: John Gilbert, Joan Crawford, Ernest Torrence, Betty Compson, Bert Roach, Eileen Percy, Edward Earle, Tom O'Brien, Harvey Clark.

CREDITS: From the play by William Anthony McGuire. Adapted by Sada Cowan. Directed by Jack Conway. Cameraman, Ira H. Morgan. Running time, 85 minutes.

SYNOPSIS

Jerry Fay (John Gilbert) is a daredevil motorcycle rider whose girl friend is stolen by rumrunner Red McCue (Ernest Torrence). Jerry determines on revenge, and decides to beat McCue at his rumrunning, hijacking game. They compete for women and easy money all over the globe, from Singapore to Buenos Aires, and while their illegal operations are separate, their paths invariably seem to cross. In Spain they are gunrunners; in Holland they are diamond smugglers. Then Jerry and McCue, each with his own separate boat and outfit, move on to the even more exciting (for them) occupation of sneaking liquor into the United States, past the Volstead Act watchdogs. In their everlasting competition for women, Jerry is always the winner and McCue, ever the bad loser, grows more and more resentful, especially after Jerry involves McCue in some sharp practices that put the latter temporarily in prison. Jerry enjoys playing tricks on McCue, and again he is usually on top, for he believes in brain and McCue in brute force. Soon both men are fighting, and racing from, Coast Guard cutters. Jerry seizes the coastal home of Jane (Joan Crawford) and plans to use it as a storehouse for rum cargoes. Jane and Jerry don't hit it off well at first, and when she threatens to turn him over to the police, Jerry kidnaps both Jane and her weakling fiancé, John Burton (Edward Earle), shanghaiing them on his rum boat. McCue pursues Jerry in his own craft, and Jerry, mistaking McCue's altered vessel for a heavily armed revenue cutter, permits the McCue party to board. McCue's resentments against Jerry have now reached the boiling point; a gun battle between them ensues, with Jane, who has by now fallen in love with Jerry, hiding below. McCue and Jerry continue to shoot it out, and both are fatally hit. Jerry dies in Jane's arms.

What the critics said about
TWELVE MILES OUT

Mae Tinee in the Chicago Tribune

Joan Crawford's Jane is a character played with charm, force and restraint.

Robert E. Sherwood in Life

It is an amusing, exciting picture, well played by Mr. Gilbert, Ernest Torrence and Joan Crawford, and competently directed by Jack Conway.

In the New York Review

Joan Crawford is lovely as Jane, and though her part affords her little variety, she makes a lot out of it, and scores a pronounced success.

With John Gilbert

With Edward Earle

Spring Fever

A Metro-Goldwyn-Mayer Picture

(1927)

CAST: William Haines, Joan Crawford, George K. Arthur, George Fawcett, Eileen Percy, Edward Earle, Bert Woodruff, Lee Moran.

CREDITS: From the play by Vincent Lawrence. Scenario by Albert Lewin and Frank Davies. Directed by Edward Sedgwick. Titles by Ralph Spence. Cameraman, Ira H. Morgan. Running time, 60 minutes.

SYNOPSIS

Jack Kelly (William Haines), a shipping clerk, is a golf whiz. His boss, Mr. Waters (George Fawcett), takes up with Jack when he learns of his prowess at the "gentleman's sport," because he hopes to get valuable pointers. Mr. Waters brings Jack to his exclusive country club and introduces him around as his nephew. Soon Jack is all over the club, dressed in loud sports togs and making like one of the millionaires. Everyone falls for his bluff that he is heir to a large fortune, including Allie Monte (Joan Crawford), a rich girl who has become a golf enthusiast. Allie's boyfriend, snobbish Eustace Tewksbury (George K. Arthur) is fed up with Jack's pretensions and annoyed at his involvement with Allie. Jack and Allie fall in love and Jack proposes. Allie pretends she has lost all her money but accepts the proposal, and they are married. Once he is her husband, Jack confesses that he is just a shipping clerk, whereupon Allie walks out on him. But Jack decides that he doesn't want to go back to Mr. Waters' factory. Instead, he turns golf pro and takes part in a championship tournament. The prize: $10,000. Allie comes to watch him play, and roots for him to win. He does. She forgives him, tells him she isn't rich, after all, and they are reconciled.

What the critics said about SPRING FEVER

Regina Cannon in the New York American

The rich young woman who plays at golf and with Mr. Haines is Joan Crawford. Although hers is a walk-through role, Joan manages to make her picture presence felt, and looks as lovely as usual.

Abel Green in Variety

Golf theme is put on a bit too thick. Despite the pleasant qualities of the plot and production, there's too much stance and niblick to *Spring Fever* for it to bogey with the general run of film fans. Haines is a likable personality and should travel far. This picture, however, will not help him much. The players do well all around and Ralph Spence's titles contribute effectively on the comedy end, but the director, Sedgwick, could not cope with a weak theme.

With William Haines

With William Haines

West Point

A Metro-Goldwyn-Mayer Picture

(1928)

CAST: William Haines, Joan Crawford, William Bakewell, Neil Neely, Ralph Emerson, Edward Richardson, Baury Bradford Richardson, Leon Kellar, Major Raymond G. Moses, Corps of Engineers, USA, Major Philip B. Fleming, Corps of Engineers, USA.

CREDITS: From the story by Raymond L. Schrock. Directed by Edward Sedgwick. Cameraman, Ira H. Morgan. Titles by Joe Farnham. Editor, Frank Sullivan. Running time, 80 minutes.

SYNOPSIS

Bruce Wayne (William Haines) is a brash youth with plenty of money. Flip and spoiled, he decides to enter West Point. His arrogance irritates his fellow cadets, and upperclassmen bear down heavily on the hazing. But the indefatigable Bruce is soon proving himself on the football field, where he runs wild in scrimmages, winning both anger and admiration from his teammates. Meanwhile, Bruce aims to be first on the romantic front also, and pursues Betty Channing (Joan Crawford), daughter of a hotel proprietor, who finds Bruce's outsized ego hard to take. Soon Bruce's football prowess is making the sports headlines and it goes to his head. When he is benched as discipline, he gives out a newspaper interview charging favoritism. For this Bruce gets bawled out by the coach, whereupon he yells, "To hell with the Corps!" A student committee meets to silence him, but he is saved by his faithful, hero-worshipping roommate, "Tex" McNeil (William Bakewell), who pleads for another chance for him. Bruce tenders his resignation to the Superintendent of the Academy, but later, just before the team leaves for the Army-Navy game, he has a change of heart and asks for another chance. Although the entire squad is disgusted with him, he is allowed back on the team. Though injured severely during the game, he manages to rescue his team from the 3-0 score and wins the game for Army. Afterwards, the happily victorious but spiritually chastened Bruce apologizes to his teammates and is reunited with Betty. The future looks bright.

What the critics said about WEST POINT

In Photoplay

Following closely upon DeMille's *Dress Parade*, we are compelled to note the similarity between the two pictures. Both make desperate efforts to correctly portray "the spirit of the Corps," and both succeed. Bill Haines' starring vehicle is a comedy drama and treats everything in a humorous vein in the beginning, getting many laughs. It winds up with the Army-Navy game. Joan Crawford is Bill's sweetheart.

In Film Daily

Bright and breezy comedy skit involving the cadet maneuvers at West Point and in particular the affairs of a wisecracking "plebe." William Haines the chesty "Mr. Dumbjohn" who gets some of the starch taken out of him before the end. Joan Crawford the girl. William Bakewell in a first-rate bit as hero's buddy.

With William Haines and unidentified player

With William Haines

Rose-Marie

A Metro-Goldwyn-Mayer Picture

(1928)

CAST: Joan Crawford, James Murray, House Peters, Creighton Hale, Gibson Gowland, Polly Moran, Lionel Belmore, William Orlamond, Gertrude Astor, Ralph Yearsley, Swen Hugo Borg, Harry Gribbon.

CREDITS: From the operetta by Otto Harbach and Oscar Hammerstein II. Scenario by Lucien Hubbard. Directed by Lucien Hubbard. Cameraman, John Arnold. Editor, Carl F. Pierson. Running time, 70 minutes.

SYNOPSIS

Rose-Marie (Joan Crawford) is French Canadian, a native of the mountains. She alternates between wildcat fierceness and purring cuteness, and captivates all the men in the trading post. Sergeant Malone (House Peters), a Canadian Mountie, is in love with her. So is Etienne Doray (Creighton Hale), effeminate son of the post's most prominent citizen. Rose-Marie loves neither of them, and steers her usual independent course. Jim Kenyon (James Murray), a mysterious soldier of fortune, drifts into the post with the trappers. Rose-Marie and Jim meet and the attraction between them is instantaneous and mutual. Shortly they are in love. Then Jim is accused of murdering a trooper. He breaks out of prison and flees down the river. To save Jim from a pursuing posse, Rose-Marie agrees to marry Etienne, who has promised to use his influence to see that Jim is not caught and tried. Meanwhile, the real murderer, Black Bastien (Gibson Gowland), is also fleeing down the river. Sergeant Malone goes in pursuit, accompanied by a posse of traders and other troopers, and is killed by Black after Black has held the Mountie's party at bay for some time in a mountain cabin. Jim is wounded in the shoulder in a gun battle with Black and flees down the rapids. Black is eventually overtaken and captured, and Jim is finally exonerated of the trooper's murder. Jim and Rose-Marie plan a future together.

What the critics said about ROSE-MARIE
Edgar Waite in the Los Angeles Examiner

Rose-Marie, divested of the musical comedy flavor in which it was last seen here, turns out to be a drama with quite a lot of suspense. Which is something that you hardly ever expect a musical comedy to grow up to. . . . Miss Crawford, who looks astonishingly like Pauline Frederick, does rather a fine piece of work. There is depth to her portrayal, though once or twice she may oversentimentalize.

With House Peters

J. G. in the St. Paul Pioneer Press

Joan Crawford, one of the most admired of the new leading women, has the title role. This is about the first time that she has been permitted to be anything but statuesque and patrician. She changes her character with a vengeance, flinging herself fiercely into the wildcat passions of the role of the French Canadian girl and also into the purring cutenesses it calls for. She is pleasant to look at in both phases.

In Photoplay

Exciting fights and daring escapes. An excellent cast with Joan Crawford a charming Rose-Marie, the daughter of the northern icebound country, who warms the hearts of all the men around her. The fur traders bring a newcomer, Jim Kenyon, played by James Murray, who, although hunted by the police, is so lovable and so daring that Rose-Marie cannot forget him. It's a little complicated but offers suspense.

With James Murray

With James Murray

Across to Singapore

A Metro-Goldwyn-Mayer Picture

(1928)

CAST: Ramon Novarro, Joan Crawford, Ernest Torrence, Frank Currier, Dan Wolheim, Duke Martin, Edward Connelly, James Mason.

CREDITS: From the story by Ben Ames Williams. Continuity by E. Richard Schayer. Directed by William Nigh. Cameraman, John Seitz. Editor, Ben Lewis. Running time, 78 minutes.

SYNOPSIS

Joel Shore (Ramon Novarro) is the youngest of four seafaring brothers of the clipper ship era. Joel and a neighbor's daughter, Priscilla Crowninshield (Joan Crawford), have been in love since childhood. Joel's oldest brother, Mark (Ernest Torrence), is also deeply in love with Priscilla, and on the eve of his sailing for the Orient, Mark has his engagement to Priscilla announced in the village church without having obtained her expressed consent. Joel is to go with Mark to sea—his first voyage. Priscilla is cold in her farewells to Mark at the wharf, and when the ship gets far out to sea, Mark, embittered by the realization that Priscilla doesn't return his love, broods about it and begins drinking heavily. Once arrived in Singapore, Mark goes on a wild spree and through the machinations of mate Finch (James Mason) Mark is deserted in Singapore while Finch assumes command of the ship, brings it back to New England, and maintains to the townspeople, (who find the innocent Joel in irons in the ship's hold), that Joel deserted Mark and left him to die. Joel gets free and, blaming Priscilla for Mark's predicament, seizes the ship and takes her back to Singapore, firm in the belief that his brother is still alive and can be rescued. Joel and his men find Mark crazed with drink, and a fight ensues. Once they get back to the ship, the crew mutinies and Mark, realizing that Joel is about to be killed, comes to his senses and leads the fight against the conspirators. Although Mark is the winner and restores order, he dies shortly afterwards from his wounds. Joel goes back to New England—and to Priscilla, who has been waiting for him longingly.

What the critics said about ACROSS TO SINGAPORE

In Photoplay

Don't try to follow the intricacies of this plot—just keep in mind that the turmoil of villainy and the sea will not overcome either Ramon Novarro or Joan Crawford. Ernest Torrence, as a horny-fisted old salt, dismisses formality and announces his engagement to the girl without consulting her. Crafty Chinese complicate matters with mutiny, dope dens and attempted seduction. Recommended as a stimulant.

In Film Daily

Ramon Novarro miscast as tough sea dog. Should have played him up on the Romeo stuff. Joan Crawford petite and always an alluring picture. Ernest Torrence dominates in strong characterization.

With Ernest Torrence

The Law of the Range

A Metro-Goldwyn-Mayer Picture

(1928)

CAST: Tim McCoy, Joan Crawford, Rex Lease, Bodil Rosing, Tenen Holtz.

CREDITS: From the story by Norman Houston. Scenario by E. Richard Schayer. Directed by William Nigh. Cameraman, Clyde DeVinna. Titles, Robert Hopkins. Editor, Dan Sharits. Running time, 60 minutes.

SYNOPSIS

Jim Lockhart (Tim McCoy), a ranger, and the "Solitaire Kid" (Rex Lease) are brothers but are not aware of it. The Kid is now a notorious bandit, while Jim upholds law and order. Years before, while traveling westward as children with their mother (Bodil Rosing), the brothers were separated during the Indian warfare and raised in different environments. Twenty years later, it is Jim Lockhart's assignment to put an end to the nefarious career of the Kid, who is ravaging the West, robbing and murdering. Jim's girl, Betty Dallas (Joan Crawford), while traveling in a stagecoach, is held up by the Kid, who falls for her. Later, she notices that Jim has a tattoo similar to one she has seen on the bandit. Now that they find themselves competitors for the girl as well as natural enemies, the warfare between Jim and the Kid steps up. Complications are provided by a mammoth prairie fire which threatens many lives. Jim and the Kid finally get to close quarters and engage in a gun battle in which the Kid is fatally wounded. Jim has learned of their relationship by now, and the final scene reunites the dying Kid with his mother and Betty while Jim stands by sorrowfully.

What one critic said about LAW OF THE RANGE

In Photoplay

If Tim McCoy has ambitions to become a Bill Hart, he makes a good start in this picture. With the help of his white horse, the "Boy Bandit," empty guns and a mammoth prairie fire, he gives us a picture which is not only a thriller but holds unusual heart interest. Joan Crawford as the sweet old-fashioned girl fires the protective instincts of both bandits and rangers; Rex Lease is the youthful robber; and Bodil Rosing plays the yearning mother.

With Rex Lease and Tim McCoy

Joan Crawford

Four Walls

A Metro-Goldwyn-Mayer Picture

(1928)

CAST: John Gilbert, Joan Crawford, Vera Gordon, Carmel Myers, Robert Emmet O'Connor, Louis Natheaux, Jack Byron.

CREDITS: From a story by Dana Burnet and George Abbot. Continuity by Alice D. G. Miller. Directed by William Nigh. Cameraman, James Howe. Titles, Joe Farnham. Editor, Harry Reynolds. Running time, 60 minutes.

SYNOPSIS

Benny (John Gilbert) is the leader of the gang in his East Side neighborhood. Frieda (Joan Crawford) is his moll. Convicted of murdering a rival gang leader, Benny is sent to prison. There he reforms his ways. Meanwhile, he gets moral support from his God-fearing mother (Vera Gordon). Bertha (Carmel Myers) is a plain-featured but virtuous young neighbor of his mother's who befriends her while he is in prison. Bertha is in love with Benny but conceals her feelings. Monk (Louis Natheaux), formerly Benny's right-hand man, has assumed leadership of the gang during his absence. He has also taken over Frieda. After four years, Benny is freed and returns to his mother's flat. Monk stops by to ascertain Benny's current attitude. Monk is assured by Benny that he is now welcome to both the gang leadership and the girl. Benny, it appears, has permanently reformed. Frieda, feeling slighted, tries to win back Benny. He tells her he no longer wants her. Refusing to take no for an answer, Frieda lures Benny to her flat, and makes advances to him. He tells her off and leaves. Benny then goes to Bertha and proposes marriage, but Bertha feels that Benny still loves Frieda and she refuses him. Benny is preoccupied by thoughts of Frieda and yearns for the old excitement. He goes to a party given by Monk. Frieda is there and pretends love for Monk in order to make Benny jealous. Monk

and Frieda announce their engagement at the party. Shortly after, a rival gang breaks in on them. Benny instinctively assumes command and rallies the gang to self-defense, over Monk's protestations. As the rival gang invades the premises, Benny flees by the roof with Frieda in his arms. An enraged Monk follows them to the roof, but falls accidentally to his death. Benny is at first suspected of Monk's murder but is later cleared.

What the critics said about FOUR WALLS

In Variety

Another underworlder, well done and with John Gilbert, Joan Crawford and Robert Emmet O'Connor in three great roles, surrounded by a one-hundred-percent cast. Gilbert, as Benny Horowitz, gangster, product of an East Side environment, plays with repression and conviction. Miss Crawford as his round-heeled frail is splendid. . . . Nigh's direction deserves commendation for its reality, restraint and knowledge of his elements.

George Gerhard in the New York Evening World

It isn't often that a supporting player manages to steal a picture right from under the nose of John Gilbert. . . . But that's what happens in *Four Walls*. . . . For Joan Crawford simply walks off with it. Not that Gilbert is very far behind her. He isn't. He gives a competent performance, just as he always does. But the story gives an infinitely better opportunity to Miss Crawford than to him. . . . [The picture] will go a long way toward lifting Miss Crawford to a point nearer the top in Hollywood circles, a point toward which she has been rapidly climbing in the last year or two.

In Photoplay

For getting down to earth with the practical sort of love-making that folks like, our hat is off to John Gilbert and Joan Crawford. John certainly takes that girl in hand, and boy, how she loves to be taken!

With John Gilbert

Our Dancing Daughters

A Cosmopolitan Production
A Metro-Goldwyn-Mayer Picture

(1928)

CAST: Joan Crawford, Johnny Mack Brown, Dorothy Sebastian, Anita Page, Nils Asther, Dorothy Cummings, Huntley Gordon, Evelyn Hall, Sam De Grasse, Edward Nugent, Eddie Quillan.

CREDITS: Story and scenario by Josephine Lovett. Directed by Harry Beaumont. Cameraman, George Barnes. Titles, Marion Ainslee and Ruth Cummings. Editor, William Hamilton. Running time, 86 minutes.

SYNOPSIS

"Dangerous Diana" (Joan Crawford) is a wild young socialite, noted for her uninhibited vivacity and love of parties. She patronizes her parents, advising them not to stay out late at their own parties. Actually, Diana is a virtuous and idealistic girl who has adopted wildness as a front. She kisses strange boys on sight and loses herself in casual competition with other girls for the affections of eligible bachelors. At one party she strips off her dress and dances in brief step-ins for her amused friends. Diana has a friend, Anne (Anita Page), who, under her baby-face is actually amoral, selfish, and immature. Child of parents equally amoral, Anne thinks nothing of arguing with her mother over gowns both want. Diana is falling in love with Ben Black (Johnny Mack Brown), heir to millions. Anne is after Ben, too. Though honestly serious about Ben, Diana continues to address herself to other boys, and Ben gets the impression that she is flighty and superficial. Anne plays the game more wisely, acts reserved and innocent. This ploy traps Ben, and he marries Anne. Soon, however, they are bickering, and Ben gradually comes to realize that it is Diana he has loved all along. Anne grows ever more loose in her conduct, dates another man, comes to a party drunk, confronts Ben and Diana, and publicly accuses them of misconduct. Diana, who has realized by this time that she lost Ben originally because she didn't reveal her true self in time, is deeply hurt. Ben, thoroughly disenchanted, decides to leave Anne. Diana tells Ben she loves him, that she has changed. Anne, drunk, tumbles down a flight of stairs to her death. Diana and Ben, sobered by recent events, look ahead to a future together.

What the critics said about
OUR DANCING DAUGHTERS

Bland Johaneson in the New York Mirror

Joan Crawford, as the girl who was free and wild but maintained her ideals, does the greatest work of her career. She has a typical Clara Bow role and she gives Clara a lively run around for

Joan Crawford

With Johnny Mack Brown

With Eddie Quillan, Johnny Mack Brown, and unidentified player

Joan Crawford and Johnny Mack Brown

With Dorothy Sebastian and Anita Page

With Dorothy Sebastian

first honors as a modern flap. Joan has beauty, charm and more refinement than the trim-legged Bow. She makes you believe she's straight even through the torrid, questionable scenes she is required to play. She also shows a snappy Bow figure and she can dance a mean varsity drag.

In the New York World

Of Miss Crawford it may be predicted that in case her managers continue to find just such breezy little comedies for her she will realize what apparently has been her ambition for at least two years, and get going as a star in her own right. She has good looks, sprightliness, intelligence and a good sense of humor. She dances with great grace and versatility and she knows when—and how—to call a halt.

Dream of Love

A Metro-Goldwyn-Mayer Picture

(1928)

CAST: Joan Crawford, Nils Asther, Aileen Pringle, Warner Oland, Carmel Myers, Harry Reinhardt, Harry Myers, Alphonse Martell, Fletcher Norton.

CREDITS: From the play "Adrienne Lecouvreur" by Eugene Scribe and Ernest Legouve. Continuity by Dorothy Farnum. Directed by Fred Niblo. Cameramen, Oliver Marsh, William Daniels. Titles, Marion Ainslee, Ruth Cummings. Editor, James MacKay. Running time, 65 minutes.

SYNOPSIS

Prince Mauritz (Nils Asther) is the heir to a Middle European kingdom. His father, the king, had been deposed by the current dictator, a duke (Warner Oland). The prince is kept on tenterhooks by the duke, who refuses him any actual powers. Mauritz fritters away the time in love affairs with a countess (Carmel Myers) and the duke's wife (Aileen Pringle), who is in love with Mauritz and plans to betray her husband and place Mauritz on the throne, with herself as his queen. Mauritz visits a traveling circus and meets one of the performers, a gypsy girl named Adrienne (Joan Cawford). He takes her home with him and makes love to her. Because of his difficult position, Mauritz, who feels a genuine love for Adrienne, decides that he cannot press his suit; he later sends her a farewell note via his friend, the Baron (Harry Myers). The Baron tactlessly adds a bank note to the letter. This hurts the feelings of Adrienne, who has fallen in love with Mauritz. She goes away feeling that the prince regards the brief affair as just another sordid experience. She cannot stop loving him, however. Years go by. Adrienne works hard at her career and in time becomes a famous actress, the toast of Europe. She returns to Mauritz's capital in a play that in its plot parallels closely their brief, tragic romance of years before. Mauritz sees her in the play and is captivated all over again. He breaks a date with the duchess to take Adrienne to dinner; the duchess, maddened by jealousy, plots Mauritz's destruction. The duke also plots against him and Mauritz finds himself in front of a firing squad—which fires in the air. Mauritz has been saved by a revolution. King at last, he and Adrienne are happily reunited.

What the critics said about
DREAM OF LOVE

In the New York Sun

Miss Crawford was not directed as well as usual, and as a result was not at her best, but *Dream of Love* is probably not the right material

With Nils Asther

With Nils Asther

for such a fresh and vital actress as she customarily is. Any coming American star is liable to wither in Graustark.

Irene Thirer in the New York News

There are some really interesting things in *Dream of Love*. Too bad that bad editing and a set of ludicrous titles should send it down into the two-star class when it might easily have made a three-star rating if more care had been taken. For instance, photography is altogether lovely. Fred Niblo's productions always boast a rare charm on that score, and this is no exception. Niblo and his cameramen work hand in hand. Joan Crawford, Aileen Pringle and Carmel Myers, three beautiful ladies of the cinema, look their best in *Dream of Love*, even if they don't quite have the histrionic chances that they should.

In the New York Times

Joan Crawford is charming as the humble singer who wins stage laurels and subsequently admits her love for the prince.

The Duke Steps Out

A Metro-Goldwyn-Mayer Picture

(1929)

CAST: William Haines, Joan Crawford, Karl Dane, Tenen Holtz, Eddie Nugent, Jack Roper, Delmer Daves, Luke Cosgrave, Herbert Prior.

CREDITS: From the story by Lucien Cary. Adapted by Raymond Schrock and Dale Van Every. Directed by James Cruze. Cameraman, Ira H. Morgan. Titles, Joe Farnham. Editor, George Hively. Running time, 62 minutes.

SYNOPSIS

Duke (William Haines), a millionaire's son who wants to be a champion boxer and has fought a number of engagements, happens to see a pretty co-ed, Susie (Joan Crawford), who takes his fancy. So he enrolls at her college under an assumed name. While there, he is something of a mystery man, due to his unusual behavior, his chauffeur, and houseful of servants. No one at the college knows he is a professional boxer, and he is not sure of it himself when, to show off, he challenges the school champion and gets beaten because he's off in his training. Duke's defeat loses him the respect of Susie, so he begins to train again in earnest. Susie has had a feeling for Duke since they first met in a roadhouse, where he had defended her against molesters. Barney (Karl Dane) is Duke's combination trainer and chauffeur. Jake (Tenen Holtz) is his manager. Jake tries to get rid of Susie by telling her Duke is in love with and engaged to a New York chorus girl. Whereupon Susie freezes Duke out. Meanwhile, Duke is training carefully for the championship bout to be held in San Francisco. Susie and other students listen to the bout over the radio, and it is not until then, that she learns that Duke, who wins the fight, is her college suitor. The misunderstanding over Duke's alleged engagement to the chorus girl is straightened out, and Duke and Susie resume romantically.

With William Haines

What the critics said about
THE DUKE STEPS OUT

Harry Mines in the Los Angeles Daily News

Haines, always a charming and breezy comedian, outdoes many of his past efforts in this clever tale of a pugilist who falls for a college beauty. He scores tremendously in every sequence, particularly in those with Joan Crawford. Miss Crawford is as gorgeous as ever, and offers a vivid performance.

In Photoplay

Another cream puff for the antics of the Metro-Goldwyn playboy Billy Haines. . . . A lightweight, friends, but amusing.

Hollywood Revue of 1929

A Metro-Goldwyn-Mayer Picture

(1929)

CAST: Conrad Nagel, Bessie Love, Joan Crawford, William Haines, Buster Keaton, Anita Page, Karl Dane, George K. Arthur, Gwen Lee, Ernest Belcher's Dancing Tots, Marie Dressler, Marion Davies, Cliff Edwards, Charles King, Polly Moran, Gus Edwards, Lionel Barrymore, Jack Benny, Brox Sisters, the Albertina Rasch Ballet, Natacha Natova and Company, The Rounders, Norma Shearer, John Gilbert, Laurel and Hardy.

CREDITS: Dialogue by Al Boasberg and Robert Hopkins. Producer, Harry Rapf. Director, Charles F. Reisner. Cameramen, John Arnold, Irving G. Reis, and Maximilian Fabian. Art Directors, Cedric Gibbons and Richard Day. Music and lyrics by Gus Edwards, Joe Goodwin, Nacio Herb Brown, Arthur Freed, Dave Snell, Louis Alter, Jessie Greer, Ray Klages, Martin Broones, Fred Fisher, Jo Trent, Avy Rice, Ballard MacDonald. Orchestra and musical score by Arthur Lange. Costumes, David Cox. Dances and ensembles by Sammy Lee. Editor, William Gray. Running time, 82 minutes.

SYNOPSIS

A revue without a plot, the film features such acts as Norma Shearer and John Gilbert playing the balcony scene from *Romeo and Juliet* and later spoofing it; Marie Dressler singing "I'm the Queen," supported by Polly Moran; Conrad Nagel (one of the two masters of ceremonies, the other being Jack Benny) singing "You Were Meant for Me"; Buster Keaton in a "Salome" dance; the Albertina Rasch Ballet; Marion Davies singing "Tommy Atkins" and doing a tap dance atop a huge drum; Cliff ("Ukelele Ike") Edwards singing "Singin' in the Rain,"; Beth Laemmele dancing the "Tableau of Jewels"; Laurel and Hardy doing their magician act; Charles King singing "Your Mother and Mine"; Charles King, Cliff Edwards, and Gus Edwards singing "Charlie, Ike and Gus," followed by Marie Dressler, Polly Moran, and Bessie Love singing "Marie, Polly, and Bess." Also 150 chorus girls doing various numbers and turns, sketches and blackouts, and ensemble work similar to those produced by Florenz Ziegfeld on the stage. *Plus* Joan Crawford assuming the Helen Morgan on-the-piano posture and singing "I've Got a Feeling for You" to an attentive male quintet. Later Joan does a dance.

What the critics said about
HOLLYWOOD REVUE OF 1929

Mark Hellinger in the New York Daily News

If this film doesn't catch on like wildfire, I am Calvin Coolidge's old electric horse. As an example of what the talking film has done to the legitimate theatre, this *Hollywood Revue* is pretty nearly the last word. I urge Flo and Earl and George and Lee and Jake to take a look at it as soon as possible. It will give them plenty to think about.

Eleanor Barnes in the Los Angeles News

Joan Crawford's popularity with the collegiate crowd is understandable. Joan is the spirit of youth. And her manner of singing "I've Got a Feeling for You"—coupled with her dancing to music furnished by the Biltmore quartet, was a radium drop for the bill.

Singing. Accompanist unidentified

With Douglas Fairbanks, Jr.

Our Modern Maidens

A Metro-Goldwyn-Mayer Picture

(1929)

CAST: Joan Crawford, Rod LaRocque, Douglas Fairbanks, Jr., Anita Page, Edward Nugent, Josephine Dunn, Albert Gran.

CREDITS: Story and screenplay by Josephine Lovett. Produced by Hunt Stromberg. Directed by Jack Conway. Cameraman, Oliver Marsh. Titles, Ruth Cummings, Marion Ainslee. Editor, Sam S. Zimbalist. Running time, 70 minutes.

SYNOPSIS

Billie Brown (Joan Crawford), daughter of B. Bickering Brown (Albert Gran), a wealthy motor magnate, is in love with Gil (Douglas Fairbanks, Jr.) and they plan to be married when Gil's diplomatic appointment is finalized. To hurry up the marriage, Billie visits Abbott (Rod LaRocque), a diplomat with political connections, and asks him to speed up Gil's appointment. Billie and Abbott get to know each other and soon they are in love, but she feels duty-bound to marry Gil. Meanwhile, however, Gil has come to know Kentucky (Anita Page), Billie's pert houseguest from the hinterlands, and a deep attraction grows between them. Soon after, they make love; later, Kentucky finds herself pregnant. Gil, not knowing this and not realizing that Billie has also fallen in love with someone else, decides that he must do his duty and marry Billie, though he loves Kentucky. The wedding goes through on schedule, but just before Billie and Gil start out on their honeymoon, Kentucky reveals to Billie that she and Gil love each other, and that she is pregnant. Billie leaves Gil, later goes to Abbott in South America. Gil and Kentucky plan for the future, after an annulment of Gil's and Billie's marriage is obtained. In the end, all are properly mated with the ones they truly love.

What the critics said about
OUR MODERN MAIDENS

In Photoplay

Joan Crawford and Douglas Fairbanks, Jr., in a sequel to *Our Dancing Daughters*. Must you be told that it's a sure-fire hit?

In Variety

Story is juvenile and silly but the sort of silliness the fans gobble by the carload. . . . Miss Crawford's fans won't be disappointed, even a little bit. She wears her clothes as she always does and gives them the limit in a half-clad dance at one of her own house parties. Her pantomime is far-fetched but vivid.

With Anita Page

With Douglas Fairbanks, Jr.

With Rod LaRocque

Untamed

A Metro-Goldwyn-Mayer Picture

(1929)

CAST: Joan Crawford, Robert Montgomery, Ernest Torrence, Holmes Herbert, John Miljan, Gwen Lee, Edward Nugent, Don Terry, Gertrude Astor, Milton Farney, Lloyd Ingram, Grace Cunard, Tom O'Brien, Wilson Benge.

CREDITS: From the story by Charles E. Scoggins. Adapted by Sylvia Thalberg and Frank Butler. Dialogue by Willard Mack. Directed by Jack Conway. Cameraman, Oliver Marsh. Titles, Lucile Newmark. Editors, William Gray, Charles Hockberg.

SYNOPSIS

"Bingo" (Joan Crawford), the daughter of an oil operator, has been brought up in the wilds of South America and knows little of civilized ways. When her father is killed, she finds herself an oil heiress, worth millions. Her guardians, rough-and-ready prospectors Ben Murchison (Ernest Torrence) and Howard Presley (Holmes Herbert), decide that their wild young charge needs some polish, and they take her to New York where she can get the background and seasoning suitable to her position in the world. On shipboard, she falls in love with Andy (Robert Montgomery), a sleek, charming, and refined young man with everything to recommend him but money. Andy shortly returns Bingo's love, but his pride forces him to renege at marriage, since he feels he cannot live on her money. Ben and Howard do not approve of Andy and try to discourage his and Bingo's love affair. Once let loose in New York, Bingo justifies her nickname by socking in the jaw everyone who rubs her the wrong way. This creates problems for her guardians. Bingo's wild, impulsive, uncivilized ways shock New York society, though some tolerate her because of her money. Bingo continues to pursue Andy, who fights his love for her. Finally, Andy decides to solve the conflict by running off with another girl, Marjory (Gwen Lee). Whereupon Bingo, enraged by jealousy and frustration, reverts to her jungle ways again and shoots him in the arm. This seems to resolve matters: Bingo and Andy reconcile and make plans to be married. Ben drops his opposition to Andy as a husband for Bingo, and offers the boy a job with the oil company. Andy decides that love must take precedence over pride, and accepts.

What the critics said about UNTAMED

George E. Bradley in the New York Star

[Miss Crawford] sings appealingly, dances thrillingly as usual; her voice is alluring and her dramatic efforts in the difficult role she portrays

With Robert Montgomery

are at all times convincing.

In the Brooklyn Eagle

If *Untamed* does little else for Miss Crawford, it proves that she is an actress for whom the microphone should hold no fear. Her diction is clear and unaffected, and while there is nothing in the lines that offers her opportunity for exceptional acting, she manages to make the impulsive heroine of the story somewhat more credible than the part deserves.

Pierre de Rohan in the New York Morning Telegraph

Miss Crawford seems more than a little ill-at-ease in the trappings of a jungle hoyden and only slightly more comfortable in the equally alien antics of a Manhattan debutante. She never, therefore, makes her role seem real and I doubt whether any other actress could.

James R. Quirk in Photoplay

Just a little jungle flower getting wilder every hour. When Joan Crawford strikes oil in one of those Latin American republics she moves into a mansion and falls in love with a young engineer. He won't marry her on account of her money, so she shoots him. Then he says yes. Joan gives a grand performance. Robert Montgomery, the hero, is in for a load of fan mail.

With Ernest Torrence

With Gwen Lee, Robert Montgomery, Don Terry

Montana Moon

A Metro-Goldwyn-Mayer Picture

(1930)

CAST: Joan Crawford, Johnny Mack Brown, Dorothy Sebastian, Ricardo Cortez, Benny Rubin, Cliff Edwards, Karl Dane, Lloyd Ingraham.

CREDITS: Story and screenplay by Sylvia Thalberg and Frank Butler. Dialogue, Joe Farnham. Director, Malcolm St. Clair. Cameraman, William Daniels. Music and lyrics by Nacio Herb Brown and Arthur Freed. Editors, Carl L. Pierson and Leslie F. Wildier. Running time, 71 minutes.

SYNOPSIS

Joan Prescott (Joan Crawford) is the spoiled, willful daughter of the richest rancher in Montana (Lloyd Ingraham). Reckless and irresponsible, Joan lives only for pleasure and luxury. While traveling home to Montana from a New York jaunt, she decides on the spur of the moment to leave the train, wait for the Eastern Express and return to New York. Impatient during the wait, she wanders about and comes across the camp of Larry (Johnny Mack Brown), a handsome young cowboy who has migrated from Texas to Montana. Joan and Larry get acquainted; she forgets about the New York train and soon they are in love. They become engaged, much to the satisfaction of Joan's father, who approves of the stalwart, sensible Larry. On their wedding night there is a boisterous Western-style party for them. A fly gets into the ointment when Joan enrages her young groom by doing a torrid dance with Jeff (Ricardo Cortez). When Joan and Jeff climax the dance with a lingering kiss, Larry strikes Jeff. In a rage, Joan takes the train for New York. Larry at first decides to let her go, then changes his mind. The train is held up by a group of cowpunchers masquerading as bandits. Joan is carried off in the arms of the "bandit leader," who turns out, of course, to be Larry. It is assumed now that Joan will stay put in Montana for some time to come.

What one critic said about MONTANA MOON

Mordaunt Hall in the New York Times

An interminable, amateurish talking picture with spasmodic snatches of melody, is now sojourning at the Capitol . . . it has a musical comedy plot that most of the time takes itself only too seriously. There is little or no idea of sound perspective in its recording, and when Joan Crawford sings, her vocal efforts are equally loud, whether she is in the foreground or on a distant edge of the Montana cowboys' camp. Two or three times it seems as if the story is about to give up the ghost, but at these junctures there suddenly comes what is supposed to be a dramatic episode and the tale goes on with renewed energy. It is a production that is equipped with poor dialogue and also one that is frequently lacking in good taste. . . . Taking it all in all, the most pleasing features of this production are Miss Crawford's camel's hair coat and her jodhpur riding outfit. . . . Miss Crawford appears to enjoy her role and sometimes her acting is quite fair.

With Dorothy Sebastian

With Johnny Mack Brown

With Ricardo Cortez

Our Blushing Brides

A Metro-Goldwyn-Mayer Picture

(1930)

CAST: Joan Crawford, Robert Montgomery, Anita Page, Dorothy Sebastian, Raymond Hackett, John Miljan, Albert Conti, Edward Brophy, Hedda Hopper.

CREDITS: Story by Bess Meredyth. Screenplay, Bess Meredyth and John Howard Lawson. Additional dialogue by Edwin Justus Mayer. Directed by Harry Beaumont. Cameraman, Merritt B. Gerstad. Editors, George Hively, Harold Palmer. Running time, 74 minutes.

SYNOPSIS

Jerry (Joan Crawford), Connie (Anita Page), and Franky (Dorothy Sebastian) work as shopgirls and mannequins for a large department store. They share a cheap apartment and are disgusted with the drab, poverty-ridden pattern of their lives. Aspiring to better things, their lives take different directions. Connie and Franky tend to be on the flighty, impulsive side, but Jerry is a sensible, levelheaded type; she is determined to stay on the straight and narrow path, no matter what the cost. True to her beliefs, she rejects the advances of Tony (Robert Montgomery), the older son of the department store owner, even though she is in love with him. Connie, on the other hand, permits Tony's younger brother David (Raymond Hackett) to have an affair with her. When David drops Connie eventually in favor of a Social Registerite, Connie, in despair, kills herself. Franky

also conducts her life unwisely. She falls in love with a suave crook, Marty (John Miljan), and marries him without realizing the true pattern of his life. Shortly, Franky finds herself in a jam with the law, though she is innocent. Thanks to Jerry's cool, sensible, and resourceful head, Franky manages to extricate herself from her unfortunate alliance and get back to her mother's farm. A rueful Jerry now finds herself the sole survivor of the three little Indians who once planned to conquer the Big City. Virtue, she tells herself, is probably the sole reward she can expect, but meanwhile Tony has had a change of heart and has come to see in Jerry a girl who deserves a sincere and permanent love.

What the critics said about
OUR BLUSHING BRIDES

Lucius Beebe in the New York Times

It is all quite lamentable and would be downright depressing in its spurious elegance if it were not for the humorous and intelligent acting of Joan Crawford, who plays the part of a mannequin with enough assurance for a marchessa and enough virtue for a regiment. If the spectacle of a shopgirl carrying herself with the sophisticated aplomb of Park Avenue is not at all convincing, it is at least humorous, although it is to be doubted if the director of the film realized it.

In Photoplay

You must see Joan Crawford in those lace stepins! Swell box office picture!

Paid

A Metro-Goldwyn-Mayer Picture
(1930)

CAST: Joan Crawford, Robert Armstrong, Marie Prevost, Kent Douglass, Hale Hamilton, John Miljan, Purnell B. Pratt, Polly Moran, Robert Emmett O'Connor, Tyrell Davis, William Bakewell, George Cooper, Gwen Lee, Isabel Withers.

CREDITS: From the play "Within the Law" by Bayard Veiller. Adapted by Lucien Hubbard and Charles MacArthur. Dialogue, Charles MacArthur. Directed by Sam Wood. Cameraman, Charles Rosher. Editor, Hugh Wynn. Running time, 80 minutes.

SYNOPSIS

Mary Turner (Joan Crawford) has been sent to prison for three years for a cime of which she is innocent. While there, she makes friends with Agnes Lynch (Marie Prevost) and Polly (Polly Moran). Embittered by her unjust sentence, she plots revenge on Edward Gilder (Purnell Pratt) and District Attorney Demarest (Hale Hamilton), who put her behind bars. Released finally from prison, Mary is introduced by Agnes to Joe Garson (Robert Armstrong), an ace crook. Garson and his accomplices are making plans for fresh activities of an illegal nature, but the shrewd and enterprising Mary suggests a new idea: Since blackmailing, for instance, carries with it severe penalties, including a long prison term, why not stay within the law by working up a "heart balm" racket? Garson likes the idea and he, Mary, Agnes, and others proceed to implement it. Agnes and Mary are assigned to inveigle elderly, well-heeled philanderers into writing them love letters; then they seek "breach of promise" and "heart balm" damages through conventional legal channels. The plan prospers, and it satisfies Mary's determination to be exploitative but "safe." For she never wants to see the inside of a prison again. Her ambitions, however, continue to grow; soon she seeks to carry her ancient revenge even further by becoming the daughter-in-law of her old enemy, Gilder, without his prior knowledge. She entices Gilder's son Bob (Kent Douglass) into falling in love with her, and they are married. The plot then thickens and digresses somewhat when the police employ a decoy to spread the false news that the "Mona Lisa," thought to be reposing in the Louvre in Paris, is actually in Gilder's home. The decoy leads Joe Garson to believe that a dealer is willing to pay hundreds of thousands of dollars for the painting. Joe and his henchmen plan the heist and execute it, while the police covertly observe their methods. Mary Turner is not involved in the proceedings. The police capture Garson and his gang and through third-degree methods, which are explained at some length, get

the truth from them. At the fadeout it is indicated that Mary has come to terms with her past, lost her vengeful spirit, and will henceforth seek peace of mind.

What the critics said about PAID

In Photoplay

Just wait until you see Joan Crawford in this powerful dramatic role! The story is absorbing and Joan is simply grand!

In the New York Times

Miss Crawford and Miss Prevost are very good in their roles.

With Polly Moran and Marie Prevost

With Kent Douglass

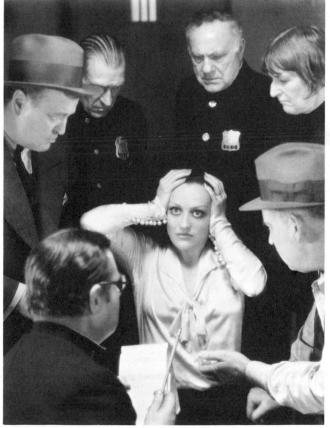

*With Robert Emmet O'Connor (left) and
unidentified group*

531-74

82

Dance, Fools, Dance

A Metro-Goldwyn-Mayer Picture

(1931)

CAST: Joan Crawford, Lester Vail, Cliff Edwards, William Bakewell, William Holden, Clark Gable, Earle Foxe, Purnell B. Pratt, Hale Hamilton, Natalie Moorhead, Joan Marsh, Russell Hopton.

CREDITS: From the story by Aurania Rouverol. Continuity, Richard Schayer. Dialogue, Aurania Rouverol. Directed by Harry Beaumont. Cameraman, Charles Rosher. Editor, George Hively. Running time, 82 minutes.

SYNOPSIS

The title here does not particularly suit the story told. The picture is loosely based on such real-life Chicago crime sensations of the time as reporter Jake Lingle's murder by underworld characters and the celebrated St. Valentine's Day massacre. Bonnie Jordan (Joan Crawford) goes to work as a cub reporter after her wealthy father, Stanley Jordan (William Holden), loses his fortune in the stock market crash. Bonnie's brother, Rodney (William Bakewell), is a shiftless, weak-willed boy who gets involved with a beer-running gang and finds himself the man at the wheel of a car used for the machine-gunning of seven members of a rival gang. Bert Scranton (Cliff Edwards), star reporter on Bonnie's newspaper, is put on the story, finds out more than he should, and is promptly murdered. The newspaper offers a $25,000 reward for the capture of the murderer. Bonnie is sent on a perilous mission: to gain the confidence of Jake Luva (Clark Gable), a Big Time gang chief who is suspected of having engineered Scranton's murder. Meanwhile, Bonnie has learned the truth about her brother's activities with the gang, and is broken-hearted and disenchanted. She learns what she needs to know about the methods of the gang, but barely escapes with her life. Throughout the film, Bonnie has been sustaining a romance of sorts with Bob (Lester Vail), an heir to millions who, during her prosperous days, had always regarded Bonnie as an emptyheaded playgirl and refused to take her seriously. After her newspaper career is a success, and she proves herself a mature and self-sufficient young woman, Bob realizes that he has always underestimated her. At the end, happiness is indicated for Bonnie and Bob, and Bonnie's weakling brother and the gang murderers have gotten their comeuppance.

What the critics said about DANCE, FOOLS, DANCE

In Photoplay

Again Joan Crawford proves herself a great dramatic actress. The story . . . is hokum, but it's good hokum and Joan breathes life into her characterization.

A. D. S. in the New York Times

Miss Crawford's acting is still self-conscious, but her admirers will find her performance well up to her standard.

With Earle Foxe and Clark Gable

Laughing Sinners

A Metro-Goldwyn-Mayer Picture

(1931)

CAST: Joan Crawford, Neil Hamilton, Clark Gable, Marjorie Rambeau, Guy Kibbee, Cliff Edwards, Roscoe Karns, Gertrude Short, George Cooper, George F. Marion, Bert Woodruff.

CREDITS: From the play "Torch Song" by Kenyon Nicholson. Continuity, Bess Meredyth. Dialogue, Martin Flavin. Directed by Harry Beaumont. Cameraman, Charles Rosher. Editor, George Hively. Running time, 71 minutes.

SYNOPSIS

Ivy Stevens (Joan Crawford) is a café entertainer in a small town. She is in love with Howard Palmer (Neil Hamilton), a shifty salesman, who later deserts her. In despair, Ivy attempts suicide by jumping from a bridge into the river. She is saved at the last moment by Carl (Clark Gable), a Salvation Army officer. Carl befriends Ivy, and under his influence she undergoes a moral reform. Tutored and encouraged by Carl, Ivy develops an interest in the work of the Salvation Army and becomes a member. Soon Ivy is on street corners with Carl, wearing the Salvation Army uniform and preaching evangelism. But then, through a fatal mischance, she encounters her old love Howard again in a hotel, and realizes that he is still in her blood. Soon Ivy has succumbed to Howard's charm all over again, and they begin an affair. Carl breaks in on them, knocks Howard down, and then informs Ivy that if she will hang on to her ideals and try again, everything will work out. We all stumble, Carl tells her, but it's picking oneself up and resuming that counts. Ivy suddenly realizes that if she had gone back to a sordid, fly-by-night, unreliable life with Howard, the path would inevitably have been downward. She comes at last to her senses, returns to the Salvation Army—and Carl, whom, she now realizes, she loves.

What one critic said about
LAUGHING SINNERS

A. D. S. in the New York Times

Miss Crawford has seldom looked so radiantly alive and beautiful; she has tempered the intense and not a little self-conscious quality of her acting without hurting her vibrant and breath-catching spirit. In the cabaret scene she gets through her dancing scenes in excellent fashion and even manages a torch song called "What Can I Do?—I Love That Man!" very commendably.

With Clark Gable

With Neil Hamilton

With Guy Kibbee (left), three unidentified players,
and (at right) Cliff Edwards and Neil Hamilton

This Modern Age

A Metro-Goldwyn-Mayer Picture

(1931)

CAST: Joan Crawford, Pauline Frederick, Neil Hamilton, Monroe Owsley, Hobart Bosworth, Emma Dunn, Albert Conti, Adrienne D'Ambricourt, Marcelle Corday.

CREDITS: From the story "Girls Together" by Mildred Cram. Continuity and dialogue, Sylvia Thalberg and Frank Butler. Directed by Nicholas Grinde. Cameraman, Charles Rosher. Editor, William LeVanway. Running time, 68 minutes.

SYNOPSIS

Socialite Valentine Winters (Joan Crawford) is a child of divorced parents. Since she has been in the custody of her father since childhood and has not seen her mother in years, she travels to Paris for a reunion. Valentine's mother, Diane (Pauline Frederick), is a chic, sophisticated expatriate who for years has been the mistress of a wealthy Frenchman, André de Graignon (Albert Conti). Valentine is kept from the truth of her mother's relationship with de Graignon, whom she thinks of as merely a family friend. Once in the French capital, Valentine finds herself involved with Tony (Monroe Owsley), a dissipated young rake who loves liquor and fast cars and is in the habit of lunching in the previous evening's tux. Tony and Valentine go for a ride in the country. Tony, driving carelessly as usual, overturns the car. He and Valentine are rescued by Bob (Neil Hamilton), a football-playing Harvardian and the son of

With Pauline Frederick

well-to-do and conservative parents. Bob and Valentine get to know each other and gradually fall in love. Eventually, Bob, with marriage in mind, brings his parents (Hobart Bosworth and Emma Dunn) to meet Diane. They are shocked when Tony breaks in boisterously with a group of his drunken friends. Then de Graignon makes a scene, and the truth about his relationship with Valentine's mother comes out in the open. Bob's parents depart in indignation, after demanding that he end his relationship with Valentine. Valentine and Diane have a heart-to-heart mother-daughter talk and achieve a new closeness and understanding. Eventually true love conquers all and Bob and Valentine go off together. Diane decides that her affair with de Graignon is affecting her peace of mind and affronting her better instincts, and she leaves him.

What one critic said about
THIS MODERN AGE

Mordaunt Hall in the New York Times

A flaxen-haired Joan Crawford is the principal figure in *This Modern Age*. . . . It is a film story which glides along merrily most of the time, but now and again it has its off-moments. . . . Nicholas Grinde, director of this picture, has done splendid work by his comedy, but his serious interludes might have been handled more effectively.

With Neil Hamilton

With Monroe Owsley

88

Possessed

A Metro-Goldwyn-Mayer Picture

(1931)

CAST: Joan Crawford, Clark Gable, Wallace Ford, Skeets Gallagher, Frank Conroy, Marjorie White, John Miljan, Clara Blandick.

CREDITS: From the play "The Mirage" by Edgar Selwyn. Adapted by Lenore Coffee. Directed by Clarence Brown. Cameraman, Oliver T. Marsh. Running time, 76 minutes.

SYNOPSIS

Marian (Joan Crawford) is a high-spirited, dissatisfied worker in a small-town paper box factory. Her routine and her relationships bore her. She is positive that life can mean more than this. Her boyfriend and co-worker Al Manning (Wallace Ford) is also determined to get out of the factory and do better things. Though not in love with Manning, Marian tolerates him for lack of anyone more appealing. A special train is accidentally delayed at the town's railroad station, and Marian encounters one of the passengers, a Manhattan opportunist, Wally (Skeets Gallagher), who increases her discontent with his tales of the Big Town. He tells her to look him up if she ever breaks away from her small-town life. Armed only with Wally's address, Marian cuts out for New York. Shorn of all illusions, she scorns a "good girl" role and aims for a rich man. Despite Wally's attempts to discourage her ambitions, she persists in her expressed aim and eventually meets

With Clark Gable

Mark Whitney (Clark Gable), a rich and influential New York lawyer whose marriage has been a failure. Whitney has political ambitions and does not want to mess them up with a divorce scandal, so instead of offering Marian marriage he sets her up as his mistress. Three years go by, and Marian, provided by Whitney with expensive clothes, a Park Avenue apartment, and some social and intellectual polish, is now "Mrs. Moreland," posing as a wealthy divorcée. Though now a woman of the world and somewhat jaded, Marian has come to love Whitney sincerely, and he her. To keep the truth of their relationship from becoming public, they maintain separate establishments. Meanwhile, Marian's old boyfriend, Al Manning, has become a moderately successful businessman. He turns up in New York, seeking Whitney's support on a road construction contract. Manning asks Marian to marry him. Comparing Manning's crudity with Mark's savior faire, Marian reneges. Whitney gets the false impression that Marian wants to marry Manning to shed her "back street" status. She lets Mark think so because she doesn't want to damage his ambitions for the governorship. But Wally reveals mercenary motives when Marian tells him the truth about her relationship with Whitney, and Marian dismisses him. Rival politicians then attack Whitney's private life, but Marian stands behind him. At the fade-out, Mar-

ian and Whitney have come to realize that the love they feel for each other is the only thing that matters.

What the critics said about POSSESSED

James R. Quirk in Photoplay

Clark Gable, the suave, worldly politician; Joan Crawford, the girl who comes to the big city to win love, wear beautiful clothes, sparkle with jewels and get very, very dramatic; lots of luxury; lots of charm; lots of smooth talk about courage and marriage and what women want—that's *Possessed*, and you really don't care if the story is old and some of the lines a little shopworn. For the Gable boy and the Crawford girl make you believe it. . . . It's the best work Joan Crawford has done since *Paid*, and Clark Gable—he's everybody's big moment. If Joan weren't so good, he'd have the picture. You'll like this. But while you're seeing it the kids should be doing their homework.

Mordaunt Hall in the New York Times

Through Clarence Brown's able direction, handsome settings and a fairly well written script, *Possessed* is a gratifying entertainment. . . . Miss Crawford adds another excellent performance to her list, and Mr. Gable delivers a performance that is nicely restrained.

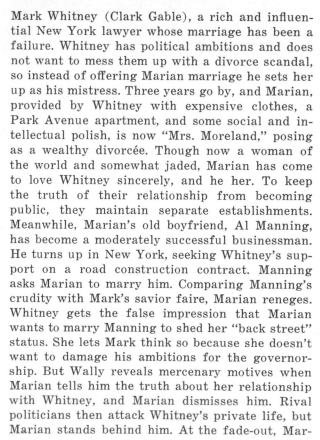

Grand Hotel

A Metro-Goldwyn-Mayer Picture

(1932)

CAST: Greta Garbo, Joan Crawford, Wallace Beery, John Barrymore, Lionel Barrymore, Lewis Stone, Jean Hersholt, Robert McWade, Purnell Pratt, Ferdinand Gottschalk, Rafaela Ottiano, Morgan Wallace, Tully Marshall, Frank Conroy, Murray Kinnell, Edwin Maxwell.

CREDITS: From the novel and play by Vicki Baum. Continuity, William A. Drake. Directed by Edmund Goulding. Cameraman, William Daniels. Costumes, Adrian. Editor, Blanche Sewell. Running time, 115 minutes.

SYNOPSIS

Flaemmchen (Joan Crawford) a stenographer at the Grand Hotel, is an ambitious girl-on-the-make. Money and luxury are her only aims, and she is not particular about where they come from. She agrees to an affair with Preysing (Wallace Beery), an industrialist, regarding him as a step up the ladder. But she finds him personally distasteful. Kringelein (Lionel Barrymore), a bookkeeper, has an incurable disease and wants to have fun during what remains of his life. He is attracted to Flaemmchen, but she feels that Preysing is the more likely foil for her ambitions. Grusinskaya (Greta Garbo), one of the guests at the Grand Hotel, is a famous ballet star who has come to perform in the city. Baron von Gaigern (John Barrymore) is an adventurer hell-bent on stealing Grusinskaya's jewels. When Grusinskaya returns dejected to her apartment after what she regards as a career failure, she surprises the Baron, who pretends he is an admirer. Gradually he is won over by her charm, and she by his eloquence, and they fall in love. The Baron tells Grusinskaya that they will meet elsewhere after she leaves the hotel, and that they will begin a new life together. Desperately in need of money, the Baron attempts to rob Preysing's suite. Preysing surprises and kills him. Flaemmchen is also in the suite, but is rescued from direct involvement by Kringelein, while Preysing is arrested. Kringelein asks Flaemmchen to go away with him and she agrees. This time, her regard for a man has become genuinely sincere, and she is hopeful, as is he, that they will find a cure for his disease from one of Europe's many specialists. Meanwhile, unaware of the Baron's death, Grusinskaya happily departs the hotel with her staff, believing that she will meet him later.

What the critics said about GRAND HOTEL

James R. Quirk in Photoplay

Here it is, the picture in which you may see Garbo, Crawford, both the Barrymores, and Wally Beery in a magnificent two hours you'll never forget. With that cast, why wouldn't it be good? Wait a minute. Vicki Baum's successful play was

With Wallace Beery

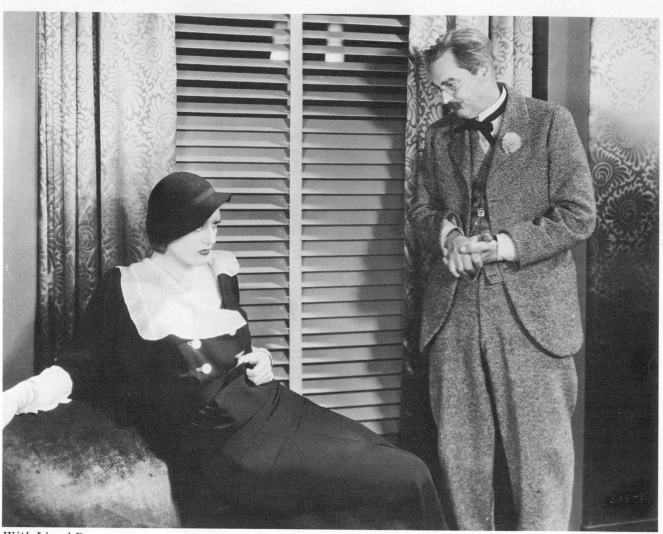

With Lionel Barrymore

With Wallace Beery and John Barrymore

With Purnell Pratt and Wallace Beery

not fool-proof, and Eddie Goulding deserves a cheer for making a smooth running story. . . . The story is not all Garbo. Joan Crawford gives excellent competition and moves up along her ladder of successes. . . . You may argue about who deserves the most praise and not get anywhere, for the picture, as a whole, steals the show. It is produced on a scale of grandeur that the stage couldn't touch. If you don't already know the story, telling it would take the edge off. You can't miss this.

Benjamin de Casseres in Motion Picture Herald

With a galaxy of stars that just have made the Milky Way sit up and keel over, the Metro-Goldwyn-Mayer production of *Grand Hotel* hits one of the high-water marks in dramatic screen plays. As drama, as comedy, as character portrayal, I rank *Grand Hotel* with the few first-class entertainments on stage or screen. So perfect, so vivid, so well done is this picture that I was not picture-conscious at all. It created an illusion of absolute reality. The acting registers one hundred percent. . . . . fairly walked out of the screen . . . Joan Crawford put all of her wiles into the stenographer who is out on the make. . . . The solidity of *Grand Hotel* not only lies in its vivid character creations and dramatic web that is so cleverly woven around these persons unknown to one another in the Grand Hotel, and who are destined to affect one another's lives, but there is an allegorical background to the whole story. Grand Hotel is the world we live in. These people are you and I. This is a great adult picture. It once more announces that the screen is rapidly coming of age.

Letty Lynton

A Metro-Goldwyn-Mayer Picture

(1932)

CAST: Joan Crawford, Robert Montgomery, Nils Asther, Lewis Stone, May Robson, Louise Closser Hale, Emma Dunn, Walter Walker, William Pawley.

CREDITS: From the novel by Marie Belloc Lown- des, Adapted by John Meehan and Wanda Tuchock. Directed by Clarence Brown. Cameraman, Oliver T. Marsh. Costumes by Adrian. Editor, Conrad A. Nervig. Running time, 84 minutes.

SYNOPSIS

Letty Lynton (Joan Crawford), a wealthy New York socialite, is vacationing in South America. There she is pursued by a handsome and persuasive international *homme fatal*, Emile Renaul (Nils Asther). Though not in love with Emile,

With Nils Asther

Letty is sufficiently intrigued to dally with him for a time; then, fed up with the sultry climate, the way of life, and Renaul, she decides to return to New York. When she tells Renaul, he objects violently and threatens her with certain letters she has written him during indiscreet moods. But Letty refuses to be deterred by threats, and with her traveling companion and maid, Miranda (Louise Closser Hale), she sails for New York. On shipboard, Letty meets Jerry Darrow (Robert Montgomery) and they initiate a shipboard romance that culminates in an engagement by the time they dock. Meanwhile, Emile has flown to New York and he shows up at the pier. His anger —and ardor—have not diminished one whit. Letty returns to the home of her mother, Mrs. Lynton (May Robson), a formidable, unsympathetic dowager type with whom Letty has never felt any closeness. Renaul comes to her mother's mansion and threatens Letty with exposure unless she goes to his apartment later that day. Letty's mother overhears their conversation. In despair, Letty goes to Renaul's apartment, taking with her some poison in a vial. Renaul is as demanding and possessive as ever, and her pleadings and arguments leave him unmoved. Letty secretly pours the poison into a wineglass, and Renaul unwittingly drinks it and dies. Letty, horrified, flees. Detectives later trace her to a party being held at the Long Island home of Jerry's parents, Mr. and Mrs. Darrow (Emma Dunn and Walter Walker), where Letty's laughter and smiles have covered her growing fears. Taken to the office of District Attorney Haney (Lewis Stone), Letty is confronted with evidence that makes her case look hopeless.

With Nils Asther

With Emma Dunn

With Robert Montgomery

At the crucial moment she is saved by an alibi concocted by Jerry, and which her mother, surprisingly, supports. Letty is discharged, is reconciled with her mother, who, she now realizes, is truly her friend, and she looks forward to a happy future with a loving and forgiving Jerry.

What the critics said about LETTY LYNTON

In Photoplay

The gripping, simple manner in which this picture unfolds stands it squarely among the best of the month. Yet there is little that is new, and no attempt at ultra-sophistication. . . . Joan Crawford as Letty is at her best. Nils Asther is a fascinating villain. Robert Montgomery gives a skillful performance; Louise Closser Hale does excellent comedy work as the maid; and Lewis Stone is fine as the district attorney. The direction, plus a strong cast, make *Letty Lynton* well worth seeing.

In the Motion Picture Herald

Almost everything one can wish for in entertainment has been injected into this superbly acted and directed production. The gowns which Miss Crawford wears will be the talk of your town for weeks after . . . and *how* she wears them!

With Walter Huston

Rain

A United Artists Picture

(1932)

CAST: Joan Crawford, Walter Huston, William Gargan, Beulah Bondi, Matt Moore, Kendall Lee, Guy Kibbee, Walter Catlett, Ben Hendricks, Jr., Fred Howard.

CREDITS: From the play "Rain," adapted by John Colton and Clemence Randolph from the story "Miss Thompson" by W. Somerset Maugham. Screenplay by Maxwell Anderson. Directed by Lewis Milestone. Cameraman, Oliver T. Marsh. Editor, W. Duncan Mansfield. Running time, 92 minutes.

SYNOPSIS

A group of steamer passengers are forced into quarantine on Pago Pago in the Samoas. There they suffer a number of physical discomforts and are disconcerted by the never-ceasing rain. Among them is a prostitute, Sadie Thompson (Joan Crawford). She is soon sought after by the members of the American military establishment stationed on the island, and with good-natured aplomb, she tries to be agreeable. But Sadie runs afoul of the fanatical missionaries Mr. and Mrs. Davidson (Walter Huston and Beulah Bondi), who pressure her to change her way of life. Reverend Davidson is especially adamant in his resolve to "reform and purify" Sadie, and her initially wry and good-natured attitude soon gives way to impatience and annoyance. Sadie is wooed by Sergeant O'Hara (William Gargan), who would also like to see her turn over a new leaf—but for different reasons. He is in love with her. Sadie cares for O'Hara, too. Meanwhile she has to contend with the demanding, powerful personality of Davidson, who finally succeeds in getting Sadie to repent and turn religious after she is threatened with deportation if she does not do

With Guy Kibbee and Matt Moore

otherwise. The hitherto cynical Sadie is also temporarily beguiled into feeling that Davidson's ideals are sincere. But her cynicism about life and people returns in full force when Davidson, giving in to his animal appetites, physically attacks her. He then commits suicide. The assumption at the end is that Sadie, though rendered more worldly wise than ever, has softened to the point where she can accept O'Hara's love.

What the critics said about RAIN

In Motion Picture Herald

Because the producers have made such a strong attempt to establish the stern impressiveness of the story, it is rather slow. In its drive to become powerful, it appears to have lost the spark of spontaneity. . . . Joan Crawford and Walter Huston are satisfactory.

In Photoplay

Joan Crawford as Sadie Thompson and Walter Huston as the stern reformer do interesting work in an adult story that never seems to grow out of date.

Abel Green in Variety

It turns out to be a mistake to have assigned the Sadie Thompson role to Miss Crawford. It shows her off unfavorably. The dramatic significance of it all is beyond her range. As for Milestone's shortcomings as an entrepreneur, apart from this being a trade surprise, the outcome is equally to be laid at his doorstep. Milestone tried to achieve action with the camera, but wears the witnesses down with words. Joan Crawford's get-up as the light lady is extremely bizarre. Pavement pounders don't quite trick themselves up as fantastically as all that. In commercial favor of *Rain* is the general repute of the theme and Miss Crawford's personal following, but the finished product will not help either.

Today We Live

A Metro-Goldwyn-Mayer Picture

(1933)

CAST: Joan Crawford, Gary Cooper, Robert Young, Franchot Tone, Roscoe Karns, Louise Closser Hale, Rollo Lloyd, Hilda Vaughn.

CREDITS: From the story by William Faulkner. Screenplay, Edith Fitzgerald and Dwight Taylor. Directed by Howard Hawks. Cameraman, Oliver T. Marsh. Editor, Edward Curtiss. Running time, 115 minutes.

SYNOPSIS

Diana Boyce-Smith (Joan Crawford), a young English playgirl during World War I, is having an affair with Claude (Robert Young), who serves as a British naval officer with Diana's brother Ronnie (Franchot Tone). Diana thinks she is enamored of Claude, but changes her mind when True Love comes along in the person of American aviator Bogard (Gary Cooper). But Bogard goes off on a flying mission and is reported killed. Whereupon the heartbroken but still resilient Diana resumes her relationship with Claude, without benefit of clergy. Her chief confidant is her brother Ronnie, but he tends to side with Claude when inevitable difficulties arise between Diana and Claude, for Ronnie feels that Diana is not being completely honest and fair with Claude. Then Bogard, who had been thought dead, turns up alive and well. Bogard, Claude, and Ronnie are thrown together and begin a friendly but barbed sea-versus-air rivalry. Scoffing at the Navy, Bogard takes Claude and Ronnie for a daredevil sky-ride. When they return safely, Ronnie challenges Bogard to accompany him to sea on Ron-

With Robert Young and Franchot Tone

With Gary Cooper

nie's motor launch, which is equipped with a single torpedo. After they have seen some stiff ocean action, Bogard has been duly convinced that there is just as much excitement on the sea as in the air. Claude is blinded in action, and as he and Ronnie know that Diana deeply loves Bogard, they decide that her happiness should not be jeopardized a second time when they hear that Bogard has offered to sacrifice his life on a suicide mission that involves sinking an enemy ship. So Ronnie and the blind Claude go out to sea in their launch and sink the vessel before Bogard has had a chance to attack it from the air. They lose their lives in the process. Bogard returns unharmed to Diana, and though relieved to be reunited, their joy is tempered by the knowledge of the frightful sacrifice of loved ones that made it possible.

What the critics said about
TODAY WE LIVE

Mordaunt Hall in the New York Times

Miss Crawford, although she never impresses one as being English, gives a steadfast and earnest portrayal. . . . [The picture] is vague and cumbersome. . . . As a drama of the war it is not precisely convincing, for coincidences play an important part in its arrangement. It is also anachronistic, particularly as regards the costumes worn by Joan Crawford.

Richard Watts, Jr. in the New York Herald Tribune Tribune

Visually, *Today We Live* is handsome, striking and genuinely dramatic, and that is not merely because Miss Crawford is photographed so beautifully. The scenes of aerial warfare are enormously effective, but such scenes have been portrayed so frequently that they have become the commonplaces of the photoplay. . . . Miss Crawford is properly effective in her role even if she doesn't seem like someone called Boyce-Smith.

Although William Faulkner is billed as the author of *Today We Live*, the picture is no devastating survey of the degeneracy of the New South, filled with murderous neurotics and pathological passions. Instead, it is a lugubrious romance of the war, replete with clipped speeches, heroic sacrifices, self-effacing nobility and many cries of "stout fellow!" As a matter of fact, it is only when one of the characters begins to play quaintly with a cockroach that you see any particular traces of the Faulkner influence at all. For the rest of the time, the work seems more akin to *Journey's End* than to *Sanctuary* or *Light in August* and devotes most of its efforts to permitting Robert Young and Franchot Tone to destroy themselves gallantly so that Gary Cooper may henceforth live happily with Miss Joan Crawford. It was my suspicion yesterday that their sacrifice was too great.

Dancing Lady

A Metro-Goldwyn-Mayer Picture

(1933)

CAST: Joan Crawford, Clark Gable, Franchot Tone, May Robson, Winnie Lightner, Fred Astaire, Robert Benchley, Ted Healy, Gloria Foy, Art Jarrett, Grant Mitchell, Maynard Holmes, Nelson Eddy, Moe Howard, Jerry Howard, Larry Fine, Sterling Holloway.

CREDITS: From the novel by James Warner Bellah. Screenplay, Allen Rivkin and P. J. Wolfson. Producer, David O. Selznick. Directed by Robert Z. Leonard. Cameraman, Oliver T. Marsh. Music by Burton Lane, Harold Adamson, Richard Rodgers, Lorenz Hart, Jimmy McHugh, Dorothy Fields. Conducted by Lou Silvers. Costumes by Adrian. Editor, Margaret Booth. Running time, 94 minutes.

SYNOPSIS

Janie (Joan Crawford) works in burlesque but is aiming at the big time, the Broadway musical stage. Despite the sleazy atmosphere in which she has worked for years, she has kept herself decent, and is determined to remain so until her wedding night. Tod Newton (Franchot Tone), a rich playboy, is enamored of Janie, but she is lukewarm toward him. Determined to win Janie through fair means or foul, Tod offers her both marriage and a job in the chorus of a Broadway musical he happens to be backing. Janie accepts the job, but demurs at marrying him; finally she promises she will become Mrs. Newton if the show is a flop. Whereupon Tod sets out to sabotage the production so as to make sure she will marry him, adopting a host of ingenious methods in the process. But Tod is up against Patch Gallagher (Clark Gable), the show's hard-boiled dance director, who is determined to make the production a success. Patch and Janie do not hit it off at first. He feels she has been forced on him because of her connection with Tod, and he harasses her in front of the rest of the cast. But she surmounts the humiliations Patch purposely inflicts, and convinces him in time that she is a talented performer. Finally, when Tod's machinations have

With Fred Astaire

almost succeeded, and it looks like the show won't go on, Janie and Patch, who are gradually falling in love, band together and manage to open. Janie's singing and dancing are the hit of the show, Tod realizes Janie loves Patch, and Patch and Janie clinch for the fadeout.

What the critics said about DANCING LADY

Richard Watts, Jr. in the New York Herald Tribune

The story . . . is almost furiously conventional in the manner in which it eludes none of the familiar clichés of its familiar school, but it is pleasantly enough played and effectively enough produced to make for pleasant if far from exciting cinema entertainment. . . . Miss Crawford, I think, is decidedly charming as the hopeful show girl, playing the role with humor, enough feeling, and with a sort of good-natured gayety which makes the heroine a rather gallant young woman. Miss Crawford's tap dance is excellent and the music is fair.

Mordaunt Hall in the New York Times

Undaunted by the scathing remarks made against it, the back-stage story rears its head more impudently than ever in the picture *Dancing Lady* which has found a home at the Capitol. It is for the most part quite a lively affair, but nevertheless one constructed along the familiar lines. The closing interludes are given over to a lavishly staged spectacle which by some stroke of magic the leading male character is supposed to put on in an ordinary-sized theatre. It looks as though it might be better suited to the Yale Bowl or Chicago's Soldiers' Field. . . . The dancing of Fred Astaire and Miss Crawford is most graceful and charming. The photographic effects of their scenes are an impressive achievement. There are several tuneful songs, such as "That's the Rhythm of the Day," "Dancing Lady," "Let's Go Bavarian," "Heigh Ho," and "Everything I Have Is Yours." Miss Crawford takes her role with no little seriousness.

With Clark Gable

With Franchot Tone

With Art Jarre

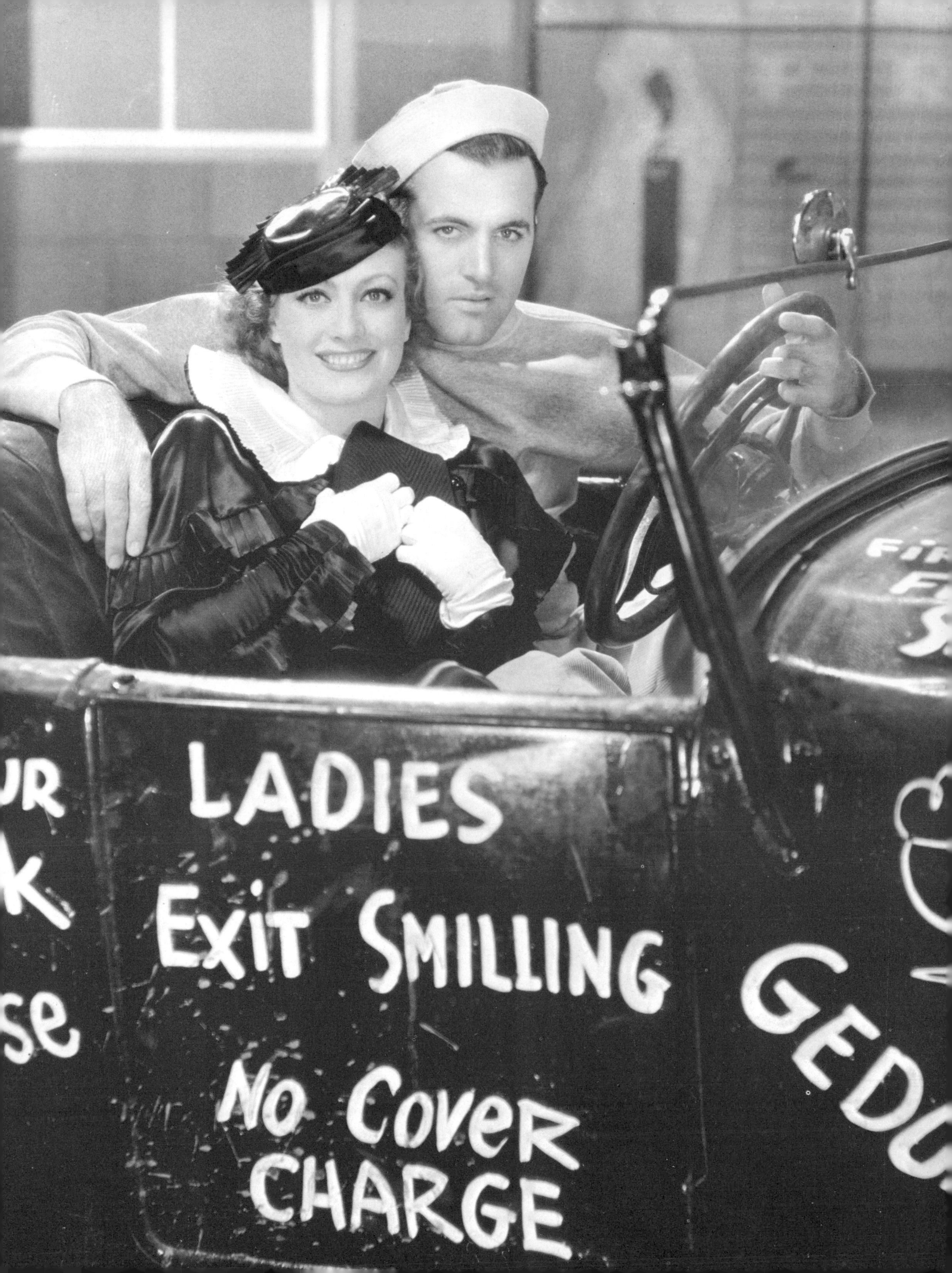
LADIES
EXIT SMILLING
NO COVER
CHARGE

Sadie McKee

A Metro-Goldwyn-Mayer Picture

(1934)

CAST: Joan Crawford, Gene Raymond, Franchot Tone, Edward Arnold, Esther Ralston, Earl Oxford, Jean Dixon, Leo Carrillo, Akim Tamiroff, Zelda Sears, Helen Ware, Helen Freeman, Leo G. Carroll. Cafe entertainers: Gene Austin, Candy, and Coco.

CREDITS: Based on the story "Pretty Sadie McKee" by Vina Delmar. Screenplay by John Meehan. Producer, Lawrence Weingarten. Directed by Clarence Brown. Cameraman, Oliver T. Marsh. Costumes by Adrian. Editor, Hugh Wynn. Running time, 88 minutes.

SYNOPSIS

Sadie McKee (Joan Crawford) is a maid in one of the wealthy houses of a small town. Her mother, the cook (Helen Ware), has been encouraging a puppy-love romance between Sadie and Michael (Franchot Tone), the "young master" of the house. Michael and Sadie are genuinely fond of each other, but Sadie is in love with Tommy (Gene Raymond), an impractical, fly-by-night type who works in a neighborhood factory. Tommy is fired from his job for dishonesty, and tells Sadie he is going to New York. Sadie feels she cannot live without him and accompanies him to New York, where she expects that Tommy will marry her. But Tommy has taken up with another girl, Dolly (Esther Ralston), and deserts Sadie at the marriage license bureau to go off with Dolly. The broken-hearted Sadie knows she will always love Tommy and will never forget him, but she determines to stay in New York and get along without him as best she can. After various ups and downs, Sadie winds up as a night-club entertainer. There she meets Brennan (Edward Arnold), an unstable millionaire with a drinking problem. Brennan tells her he cottons to her because they were both born children of cooks. Finally, Sadie marries Brennan, out of pity rather than love; her life with him is not happy because of his emotional insecurities and neurotic conduct, expressed via the bottle. Tommy has meanwhile continued the loose and sordid pattern of life which leads eventually to his death. Sadie is notified and she is with him at the end. Life seems bleak to her now. She has

money and a certain amount of social position, but she has lost the man she loved and finds herself married to another who represents a major problem. Michael, the rich young man from her home town, comes back into her life at this point, and after a number of soul-searchings and assorted vicissitudes, Sadie realizes that she and Michael are genuinely in love with each other and that her hitherto fruitless search for an enduring love has come at last to a happy ending.

What the critics said about SADIE McKEE
Mordaunt Hall in the New York Times

Clarence Brown's direction of this film is studied and in its way effective but it scarcely improves the flow of the story. There are many static interludes, a great deal of talk, which is by no means as interesting as the producers evidently thought it to be. Miss Crawford assuredly does well by her part, but even so the incidents in which she appears often are hardly edifying. It is in fact an exasperating type of motion picture.

Marguerite Tazelaar in the New York Herald Tribune

Mr. Brown has employed an emotional quality in his direction that both helps and hinders the picture. It helps in keeping the story an exciting, vivid, enkindled canvas. It hinders, in exaggerating its artifice, its confusion and its lack of logic. He has set it handsomely and photographed it well. Miss Crawford seems a bit miscast in the role of girlish innocence, but she does a competent job with Sadie, and in certain of her scenes is genuinely moving.

In the Hollywood Reporter

Swell picture . . . sure-fire audience . . . well-tailored for the talents of Joan Crawford. . . . the stuff the fans cry for . . . direction of Clarence Brown something to rave about. . . . John Meehan's dialogue expert and amusing. . . . a humdinger for the femme fans.

In Motion Picture Herald

Presenting Joan Crawford in a role uniquely adapted to her screen character, the picture is well acted. . . . Presented in a 1934 atmosphere, realistically and elaborately produced, it's the kind of show that carries definite entertainment for the modernes.

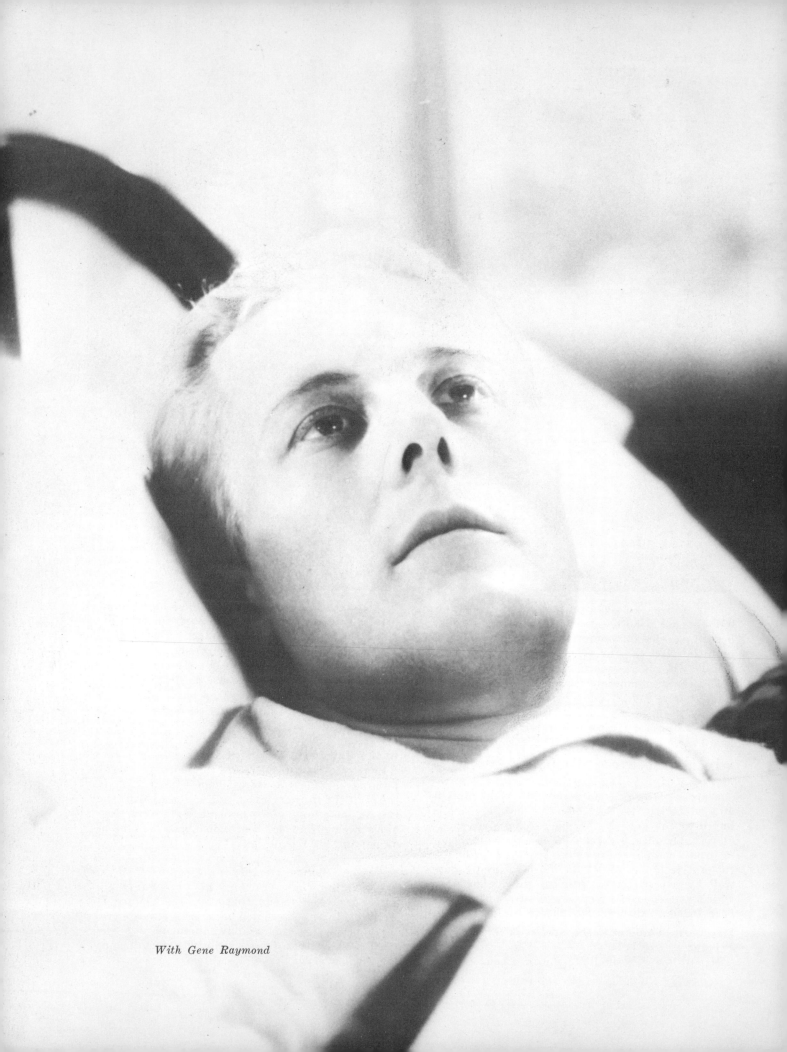

With Gene Raymond

With Clark Gable

With Otto Kruger and Clark Gable

Chained

A Metro-Goldwyn-Mayer Picture

(1934)

CAST: Joan Crawford, Clark Gable, Otto Kruger, Stuart Erwin, Una O'Connor, Marjorie Gateson, Akim Tamiroff.

CREDITS: From the story by Edgar Selwyn. Screenplay by John Lee Mahin. Produced by Hunt Stromberg. Directed by Clarence Brown. Cameraman, George Folsey. Costumes by Adrian. Editor, Robert J. Kern. Running time, 74 minutes.

SYNOPSIS

Richard Field (Otto Kruger), a wealthy steamship owner, is in love with Diane Lovering (Joan Crawford). Field's wife (Marjorie Gateson) refuses, however, to give him a divorce. Caught in an unhappy impasse, Diane takes a trip to South America and on the steamship encounters Mike Bradley (Clark Gable). Diane feels friendship and affection for Field without being truly in love with him, but her loyalty to her married suitor prevents her from allowing her initial feelings for Mike to develop. Eventually, however, Mike sweeps away her resistance and they have a passionate shipboard romance. However, the time comes for Diane to return to New York, where she learns to her surprise that Field's wife is suing for divorce after all, leaving him free to marry Diane. Because she is grateful to Field and doesn't wish to hurt him, Diane consents to a marriage and tries to forget about Mike. But Mike isn't satisfied to leave things as they are; he soon turns up in New York. Diane and Mike find they are truly and sincerely in love with each other; and the problem then arises as to how to throw themselves on Field's mercy. Field, however, is a kindly realist; he understands that youth must be served, and steps aside with good grace.

What the critics said about CHAINED

In Motion Picture Herald

The showmanship value of the entertainment elements with which this picture deals is long and solidly established. The leading players, Joan Crawford and Clark Gable, are among the foremost exponents of the type of romantic theme which is its motivation.

Richard Watts, Jr. in the New York Herald Tribune

May I say that although I expect the film to make a million dollars for its producers, it seemed to me just an earnest camera treatment of a snappy serial in one of the dressier sex magazines. . . . Since the picture doesn't even attempt to go in for credibility, no one should blame Miss Crawford or Mr. Gable for failing to give real portrayals in their romantic roles. The two stars, who certainly know their business, wisely decide to pass their time tossing charm and personality all over the place, which is obviously what the film requires for audience appeal.

M. H. in the New York Times

Miss Crawford adds to the general attractiveness of the scenes of this . . . offering by an unusually extensive wardrobe and a variety of changes in her coiffure. But when it comes to weighing the merits of the story, it must be said that it is just another suspenseless triangle. So long as Miss Crawford and Mr. Gable are in a picture, it is as inevitable as the coming of night that the characters they impersonate will not be disappointing in the end. . . . Miss Crawford gives a facile performance, and Mr. Gable is as ingratiating as ever.

With Clark Gable

With Robert Montgomery

With Robert Montgomery

Forsaking All Others

A Metro-Goldwyn-Mayer Picture

(1934)

CAST: Joan Crawford, Clark Gable, Robert Montgomery, Charles Butterworth, Billie Burke, Frances Drake, Rosalind Russell, Tom Rickets, Arthur Treacher, Greta Moyer.

CREDITS: From the story by Edward Barry Roberts and Frank Morgan Cavett. Screenplay by Joseph L. Mankiewicz. Produced by Bernard H. Hyman. Directed by W. S. Van Dyke. Cameramen, Gregg Toland and George Folsey. Costumes by Adrian. Editor, Tom Held. Running time, 82 minutes.

SYNOPSIS

Mary (Joan Crawford), Jeff (Clark Gable), and Dill (Robert Montgomery) have grown up together, and enjoy a close, continuing friendship. Jeff is in love with Mary, who thinks she is in love with Dill. Jeff returns from a European holiday to learn that Mary and Dill are about to be married. Knowing that his love for Mary is hopeless under the circumstances, he conceals it. Dill, however, is an indecisive, self-indulgent hedonist, and he leaves Mary waiting at the church. Then she learns through a telegram that Dill has run off and married his former mistress, Connie (Frances Drake). Jeff seeks to comfort the devastated Mary, whose wounds are slow in healing. Meanwhile, Dill has discovered that marriage to Connie is not a bed of roses, and that he preferred her as a mistress rather than a wife. Dill thereupon does an about-face and begins worming his way back into the affections of Mary, who is still in love with him and forgives him. Jeff, exasperated and hurt, has to stand by at all this, while smothering his own feelings. But just as it looks as though Mary and Dill will get to the altar at long last, Mary wakes up to the realization that it is Jeff she has loved all along. She so informs Dill, who takes it in good grace, knowing it is exactly what he deserves, and Mary and Jeff take a liner for Europe. Dill, determined to be a good sport, waves goodbye from the pier.

What one critic said about
FORSAKING ALL OTHERS
In Variety

On the performance end, it is one of Miss Crawford's best. She is believable throughout. That tongue-in-cheek moralizing which often marks many of her sagas is largely missing. This is just a semi-rowdy, semi-drawing room eternal triangle.

With Clark Gable

No More Ladies

A Metro-Goldwyn-Mayer Picture

(1935)

CAST: Joan Crawford, Robert Montgomery, Charlie Ruggles, Franchot Tone, Edna May Oliver, Gail Patrick, Reginald Denny, Vivienne Osborne, Joan Burfield, Arthur Treacher, David Horsley, Jean Chatburn.

CREDITS: From the play by A. E. Thomas. Screenplay by Donald Ogden Stewart and Horace Jackson. Produced by Irving Thalberg. Directed by Edward H. Griffith and George Cukor. Cameraman, Oliver T. Marsh. Costumes by Adrian. Editor, Frank E. Hull. Running time, 79 minutes.

SYNOPSIS

Marcia (Joan Crawford) is an intense young society girl who believes love is very important, and that it should be exclusively between two people and should last forever. Though attractive and sought after by many young men, including Jim (Franchot Tone), who more or less agrees with her ideas on the subject, Marcia elects to fall in love with Sherry (Robert Montgomery), a dissolute philanderer and consummate rake who changes women almost as often as he changes his shirts. But Marcia persists in believing that Sherry can be cured of his ubiquitously romantic tendencies, and she inveigles him into marrying her. Among the many women in Sherry's past and present are Theresa (Gail Patrick), Lady Diana Moulton (Vivienne Osborne), and Caroline (Joan Burfield). Jim meanwhile indicates that he loves Marcia seriously and will be glad to take her back any time she gives the word. But Marcia believes in fidelity to the marriage vows. It presently becomes obvious that Sherry does not, and when Marcia learns of his latest infidelity, she

With Robert Montgomery and Franchot Tone

With Robert Montgomery

decides to teach him a lesson he will not soon forget. Coldly and methodically, she organizes a house party made up of all the people whose lives Sherry has systematically messed up over the years. And so he is confronted with a bevy of disillusioned women and their cuckolded husbands. Then Marcia tops her "revenge" by rushing off with Jim for an ostensible extramarital affair. However, she cannot go through with it, for her standards remain despite herself. Moreover, she still loves Sherry. And Sherry, belatedly, realizes that he loves Marcia sufficiently to reform his rakish ways.

What the critics said about
NO MORE LADIES

Andre Sennwald in the New York Times

Out of the labors of the brigade of writers who tinkered with the screen play, there remain a sprinkling of nifties which make for moments of hilarity in an expanse of tedium and fake sophistication. . . . The photoplay keeps a comic drunk and a comic Englishman on the sidelines for use in those frequent emergencies when the glamour becomes lumpy. Although Donald Ogden Stewart has contributed several really funny lines, the screen play is chiefly notable for its surface shimmer, the hollowness of its wit, and the insincerity of its emotions. The sophistication of *No More Ladies* is the desperate pretense of the small girl who smears her mouth with lipstick and puts on sister's evening gown when the family is away. It ought to make a very respectable profit.

Howard Barnes in the New York Herald Tribune

Miss Crawford's portrayal of Marcia, the worldly innocent who marries a rake and almost goes away with another man when she finds her husband has been unfaithful to her, is incisive but unconvincing. The sophistication of her attitude towards matrimony and life is less a mood of her own creation than a pattern of gestures and spoken lines. She is handsome and engagingly defiant in the scene that brings together her husband's former conquests and marks her attempt to pay him back in kind for his infidelity, but on the whole hers is not a distinguished performance.

With Brian Aherne

I Live My Life

A Metro-Goldwyn-Mayer Picture

(1935)

CAST: Joan Crawford, Brian Aherne, Frank Morgan, Aline MacMahon, Eric Blore, Fred Keating, Jessie Ralph, Arthur Treacher, Hedda Hopper, Frank Conroy, Etienne Girardot, Edward Brophy, Sterling Holloway, Hilda Vaughn, Vince Barnett, Lionel Stander, Hale Hamilton.

CREDITS: Based on the short story "Claustrophobia" by A. Carter Goodloe. Developed by Gottfried Reinhardt and Ethel Borden. Screenplay by Joseph L. Mankiewicz. Produced by Bernard H. Hyman. Directed by W. S. Van Dyke. Cameraman, George Folsey. Costumes by Adrian. Editor, Tom Held. Running time, 85 minutes.

SYNOPSIS

Kay (Joan Crawford), a bored society girl who plays the New York–Connecticut circuit, takes a trip abroad and in Greece meets Terry (Brian Aherne), a young archaeologist with proletarian inclinations. Something of a trifler in matters of romance, Kay leads Terry on, and there are some affectionate moments before she returns to New York. However, Terry is a serious, studious type who believes a caress is the equivalent of a marriage proposal. He follows Kay back to America, and finds himself something of a bull in a chinashop among her snobbish, pleasure-loving society friends. Terry sneers at their polo games and tells them their lives are degenerate and that there are millions of starving poor who would find their polo ponies good enough to eat. Kay's friends all dub him Quaint, but her grandmother, Mrs. Gage (Jessie Ralph), the family matriarch, develops a liking for Terry and encourages his suit of Kay. Meanwhile Terry has to contend with such high-life denizens as Bentley (Frank Morgan), Kay's pixilated but lovable father; Gene (Fred Keating), a playboy; and Eric Blore and Arthur Treacher in their usual comic-butler impersonations. Terry continues to pressure Kay to abandon her pointless existence and help him dig up statues in the Aegean. They become engaged but have a serious quarrel just before the scheduled wedding. Terry agrees to be a gentleman and show up at the church on his wedding day to play the jilted suitor and spare Kay embarrassment. But Kay has a predictable change of heart and shows up for the ceremony after all. Whereupon years of happy archaeological expeditions together are projected.

What one critic said about
I LIVE MY LIFE

Richard Watts, Jr. in the New York Herald Tribune

[The picture] has something of the vitality that W. S. Van Dyke, its director, invariably gets into his works, but it is a pretty routine bit of story telling. If, however, you're an enthusiast for the regulation type of Crawford vehicle, you may find the work soul-satisfying. The star plays handsomely and competently.

With Frank Morgan

With Robert Taylor

With Lionel Barrymore

The Gorgeous Hussy

A Metro-Goldwyn-Mayer Picture

(1936)

CAST: Joan Crawford, Robert Taylor, Lionel Barrymore, Franchot Tone, Melvyn Douglas, James Stewart, Alison Skipworth, Louis Calhern, Beulah Bondi, Melville Cooper, Sidney Toler, Gene Lockhart, Clara Blandick, Frank Conroy, Nydia Westman, Charles Trowbridge, Willard Robertson, Ruby DeRemer, Betty Blythe, Zeffie Tilbury.

CREDITS: Based on the novel by Samuel Hopkins Adams. Screenplay by Ainsworth Morgan and Stephen Morehouse Avery. Produced by Joseph L. Mankiewicz. Directed by Clarence Brown. Cameraman, George Folsey. Art director, Cedric Gibbons. Musical score, Herbert Stothart. Costumes by Adrian. Editor, Blanche Sewell. Running time, 105 minutes.

SYNOPSIS

Peggy O'Neal (Joan Crawford) is an innkeeper's daughter in the Washington of the 1830s. The President of the United States Andrew Jackson (Lionel Barrymore) is an energetic crusader for the preservation of the Union against the encroachments of the states-righters. Washington society looks askance on him because his late wife, Rachel (Beulah Bondi), had been a backwoodswoman of crude manners who had lived with Jackson in inadvertent bigamy for years (her divorce from her first husband not having been finalized). Jackson and Peggy meet during the period he and his wife stay at the inn, and a bond is formed, of a purely platonic kind, because they have their humble backgrounds and progressive ideas (Peggy advocates woman suffrage) in common. Peggy is on intimate terms with all the Washington politicos of her time, many of whom stay at the inn of her father, Major O'Neal (Gene Lockhart). Much courted by the males, Peggy is in love with John Randolph (Melvyn Douglas), later a senator, but he rejects her. On the rebound, Peggy allows herself to be carried away by the boyish charm of a young Navy lieutenant, "Bow" Timberlake (Robert Taylor), and they are married. She doesn't remain Mrs. Timberlake for long, however, for he is killed in action. She then begins a romantic liaison with John Eaton (Franchot Tone), later a cabinet member, and this marriage turns out to be lengthy and happy. As she rises socially in Washington, Peggy encounters the opposition of the more snobbish female society leaders, but the males—including the influential statesmen—flock around because of Peggy's vivacity, intelligence, and advanced ideas. Peggy and President Jackson have an excellent rapport, and Peggy becomes an "unofficial Presidential niece" and a trusted confidante. Peggy's enemies, jealous of her influence with the President, intrigue against her and impugn her loyalty to the Union. The angered Jackson institutes an inquiry resulting in the dismissal of his cabinet members and their wives for their intrigues and slanders against Peggy. Eventually, however, Peggy makes a gallant gesture and leaves Washington rather than cause Jackson's administration any further embarrassment. However, she lingers in the memory of the President and all her sincere friends and admirers as one of the most delightful and memorable women ever to grace the national capital's social scene.

What the critics said about
THE GORGEOUS HUSSY

Howard Barnes in the New York Herald Tribune

In the title role Joan Crawford is handsome, although century-old costumes do not go well with the pronounced modernity of her personality. She makes of Peggy Eaton a straightforward and zealous figure. . . . Mr. Brown has staged the piece with a keen eye for its color and pageantry, permitting the romantic interludes to balance as they will with re-created history in a show that is rich with trappings and accented by moments of moving intensity.

Frank Nugent in the New York Times

It is our hope that some day we may come to understand why Hollywood, when it selects a colorful personality for one of its themes, almost invariably chooses to divest the hapless character of that very color which seemed to justify a screen biography, and hastens to reduce it (or him or her) to a faded stereotype which might pass for anyone. What we have here, and you might as well make the best of it, is a thoroughly romanticized biography in which Miss Crawford is gorgeous, but never a hussy. An innkeeper's daughter she may be, but that is all the women of Washington can possibly hold against her. Sweet, demure, trusting and of rather doubtful inspiration to Old Hickory . . . Miss Crawford's Peggy is a maligned Anne of Green Gables, a persecuted Pollyanna, a dismayed Dolly Dimple.

With Melvyn Douglas

Love on the Run

A Metro-Goldwyn-Mayer Picture

(1936)

CAST: Joan Crawford, Clark Gable, Franchot Tone, Reginald Owen, Mona Barrie, Ivan Lebedeff, Charles Judels, William Demarest.

CREDITS: From the story by Alan Green and Julian Brodie. Screenplay by John Lee Mahin, Manuel Seff, and Gladys Hurlbut. Produced by Joseph L. Mankiewicz. Directed by W. S. Van Dyke. Cameraman, Oliver T. Marsh. Costumes by Adrian. Editor, Frank Sullivan. Running time, 81 minutes.

SYNOPSIS

Michael Anthony (Clark Gable) and Barnabas Pells (Franchot Tone) are rival newspaper correspondents covering the European scene. Michael is always outwitting Barnabas, who despite his best efforts invariably comes in a poor second. The boys get assignments to cover a stratosphere flier, the Baron (Reginald Owen), who, it turns out, is actually a shrewd and ruthless international spy. They are commissioned also to cover the marriage of American heiress Sally Parker (Joan Crawford) to Prince Igor (Ivan Lebedeff). Sally, however, has decided she does not love Igor and wants out of the marriage. She hates newspapermen, who have hounded her every activity for years. Not knowing that Michael is a newshound, she enlists his aid in helping her escape her altar date. Michael, who is always a pushover for spontaneous larks, spirits Sally away in a stolen airplane, and soon she finds herself being dragged dizzily across the face of Europe via air, auto, and oxcart while Michael seeks to expose and corner the Baron and his espionage operatives. Barnabas ruefully tags along, getting himself thoroughly hoodwinked by Michael from London to Nice. Soon Michael, Sally, and Barnabas are themselves the prime targets of the spies, and a long tortuous game of hide-and-seek goes on, during which Michael and Sally take refuge in the endless expanses of the Palace of Fontainebleau, where they meet a batty caretaker (Donald Meek), who persuades himself that Michael and Sally are the reincarnations of King Louis and Madame de Maintenon. Meanwhile, Sally and Michael, despite their hot running battles, are gradually falling in love. They succeed in outwitting and decommissioning the spy ring. Then, after one final man-woman, grand-finale set-to, they surrender to their mutual feelings and marry. Barnabas, as usual, is odd man out.

What the critics said about LOVE ON THE RUN

J. T. M. in the New York Times

A slightly daffy cinematic item of absolutely no

With Clark Gable

With Franchot Tone

With Clark Gable

importance . . . with Joan Crawford, Clark Gable and Franchot Tone in roles that by now are a bit stale. In all good conscience, the film ought to bow, in turn, to several distinguished antecedents, for it has borrowed liberally here and there of tried and true screen devices and situations.

Howard Barnes in the New York Herald Tribune

A lot of gay nonsense has been strung together . . . a delightful addition to a season prodigal with screen comedy. The director, scenarists, and players have collaborated superbly on a fantastic and insubstantial narrative, with the result that it is almost continuously amusing and frequently hilarious . . . Miss Crawford, of the big eyes and flowing hair, turns in a surprisingly volatile and amusing performance as the heiress.

With Robert Montgomery and Frank Morgan

The Last of Mrs. Cheyney

A Metro-Goldwyn-Mayer Picture

(1937)

CAST: Joan Crawford, William Powell, Robert Montgomery, Frank Morgan, Jessie Ralph, Nigel Bruce, Colleen Clare, Benita Hume, Ralph Forbes, Aileen Pringle, Melville Cooper, Leonard Carey, Sara Haden, Lumsden Hare, Wallis Clark, Barnett Parker.

CREDITS: Adapted from the play "The Last of Mrs. Cheyney" by Frederick Lonsdale. Screenplay by Leon Gordon, Samson Raphaelson, and Monckton Hoffe. Produced by Lawrence Weingarten. Directed by Richard Boleslawski. Cameraman, George Folsey. Art Director, Cedric Gibbons. Music, Dr. William Axt. Editor, Frank Sullivan. Running time, 98 minutes.

SYNOPSIS

Fay Cheyney (Joan Crawford) is a lady Raffles who travels in high British society. Devoid of background but rich in charm and glib persuasiveness, she worms her way into aristocratic confidences at assorted houseparties, with her eye always on available jewels worn by her companions. Fay is aided and abetted in her polished schemes by Charles (William Powell), an accomplished jewel thief who poses as a butler. Lord Arthur (Robert Montgomery) dallies with Fay, who compels his admiration by exhibiting far more poise and wit than Kitty (Benita Hume) and Maria (Aileen Pringle), who are of his own class. Fay and Charles are assisted in their jewel-heist-ing schemes by other conspirators, all of them making meticulous plans for a major "take" at a fashionable weekend party in the English countryside. Fay has a unique psychology for a thief: She considers herself to be a "respectable adventuress" rather than a criminal, and feels superior to the aristocrats she robs. Her cohort Charles regards her sympathetically and tolerantly. Love letters come to light, written to Fay by Lord Kelton (Frank Morgan), and this introduces added complications. Everything eventually comes out in the open, with Fay deciding to abandon her "career" and retire to happy domesticity with Charles. Not, however, before a series of contretemps, in which Lord Arthur reveals himself as a cad and the assorted high-lifers show themselves even more human and fallible than the jewel thieves who seek to prey on them.

For Lord Kelton, in his love letter to Fay, has painted his aristocratic friends in unflattering colors. When cornered as thieves, Fay and Charles in turn make the blue-bloods squirm by threatening to submit the embarrassing letter as part of the court evidence. Whereupon an advance compromise is reached, satisfactory to all.

What one critic said about
THE LAST OF MRS. CHEYNEY

Marguerite Tazelaar in the New York Herald Tribune

Joan Crawford as Mrs. Cheyney was competent, besides giving the part considerable sympathy. . . . The picture has been staged handsomely, the musical score accompanying it is good, and the lines glitter.

With Robert Young

The Bride Wore Red

A Metro-Goldwyn-Mayer Picture

(1937)

CAST: Joan Crawford, Franchot Tone, Robert Young, Billie Burke, Reginald Owen, Lynne Carver, George Zucco, Mary Phillips, Paul Porcasi, Dickie Moore, Frank Puglia.

CREDITS: Based on the unpublished play "The Girl from Trieste" by Ferenc Molnar. Screenplay by Tess Slesinger and Bradbury Foote. Produced by Joseph L. Mankiewicz. Directed by Dorothy Arzner. Cameraman, George Folsey. Art Director, Cedric Gibbons. Music by Franz Waxman. Costumes by Adrian. Editor, Adrienne Fazan. Running time, 103 minutes.

SYNOPSIS

Anni (Joan Crawford) is a beautiful and talented, but also cynical and embittered, cabaret singer in Trieste. One of the patrons, Count Armalia (George Zucco), is a bon vivant who enjoys playing ironic games on what he calls "the wheel of life." The Count calls the suspicious Anni to his table and suggests to her that she allow him to finance two weeks for her at an expensive resort in the Tyrol where only the well-heeled and the aristocratic hibernate. Anni, whose life is drab and futureless, agrees. Decked in high-fashion gowns, she arrives at the vacation chalet posing as a rich pleasure-seeker of indeterminate background. Soon she is being pursued romantically by two men: wealthy, well-connected Rudi Pal (Robert Young) and the village postman, Giulio (Franchot Tone), a whimsical poetic type who despises materialism and the prestige rat-race. Anni is intrigued by Giulio, but fights her growing attachment to him and continues to hob-nob with Rudi and his fashionable crowd, which includes Contessa Di Meina (Billie Burke) and Admiral Monti (Reginald Owen) and his daughter Maddelena (Lynne Carver). Though the days pass pleasantly, Anni is growing nervous. She realizes that she can't continue her imposture forever, that her two weeks will soon be up, and Cinderella will have to leave the ball. Meanwhile, Rudi continues his courtship while Giulio looks on ruefully. Finally the witching hour strikes, accompanied by a denouncement in which Anni defiantly sports a red evening gown in front of Rudi's snobbish crowd. Exposed for what she is, Anni loses Rudi and the life he represents, but finds a haven in Giulio's loving arms. Giulio, it seems, had suspected her ruse from the beginning.

What the critics said about
THE BRIDE WORE RED

Howard Barnes in the New York Herald Tribune

Joan Crawford has a glamorous field day in *The Bride Wore Red.* . . . With a new hair-do and more wide-eyed than ever, she plays at being a slattern, a fine lady, and a peasant with all of the well-known Crawford sorcery. It is not entirely her fault that she always remains herself. [The film] has no dramatic conviction and little of the comic flavor that might have made it amusing though slight. Your enjoyment of it will depend on how much of Miss Crawford you can take at one stretch. . . . The direction of Dorothy Arzner is always interesting and sometimes . . . is extraordinarily imaginative, but here she has not been able to give a vapid Cinderella pipe dream more than a handsome pictorial front.

Frank S. Nugent in the New York Times

Gowns by Adrian and settings by Cedric Gibbons do not entirely conceal the underlying shabbiness of *The Bride Wore Red,* one of those seasonal rediscoveries of Cinderella which Metro-Goldwyn-Mayer turned into the Capitol yesterday. Now it has Miss Joan Crawford who puts on an emotional circus as the shoddy cabaret girl (with dreams) who has been given two glorious weeks with high society in the Tyrol and tries desperately to have the clock stopped before her witching hour strikes. . . . If anything at all, it is a woman's picture—smouldering with its heroine's indecision and consumed with talk of love and fashions. Tall talk, mostly.

With Robert Young and Franchot Tone

With Spencer Tracy

With Alan Curtis

With Spencer Tracy and Alan Curtis

Mannequin

A Metro-Goldwyn-Mayer Picture

(1938)

CAST: Joan Crawford, Spencer Tracy, Alan Curtis, Ralph Morgan, Mary Phillips, Oscar O'Shea, Elizabeth Risdon, Leo Gorcey.

CREDITS: Developed from an unpublished story by Katharine Brush. Screenplay by Lawrence Hazard. Produced by Joseph L. Mankiewicz. Directed by Frank Borzage. Cameraman, George Folsey. Costumes by Adrian. Editor, Frederic Y. Smith. Running time, 95 minutes.

SYNOPSIS

Jessica Cassidy (Joan Crawford) is a lower-class working girl in love with a small-time chiseler, Eddie Miller (Alan Curtis). Eddie asks Jessie to marry him, and though they have little money, she agrees. At their wedding supper in a restaurant, they are congratulated by a man at a nearby table, who turns out to be shipping magnate John L. Hennessey (Spencer Tracy). Hennessey's admiration for Jessie is immediately apparent, as Briggs (Ralph Morgan), the bachelor Hennessey's assistant, notes. Jessie finds married life with Eddie heartbreaking and disillusioning; in time she gets fed up with his chiseling, irresponsible ways and leaves him. She gets a job as a mannequin, modeling expensive clothes, and Hennessey comes into her life again. She is still in love with Eddie, however, or thinks she is, and for a time Hennessey's suit is not encouraged. Gradually, however, Jessie is won over by Hennessey's basic decency and lovable spirit, and she divorces Eddie, who has disappeared, and marries Hennessey. Jessie and Hennessey take a long and deeply fulfilling European vacation, then return to New York. Eddie reappears on the scene, and attempts to blackmail Hennessey and Jessie. Jessie refuses to go along with him on any of it, and rebuffs Eddie, whom she now realizes she no longer loves, and probably never loved. Hennessey, through a misunderstanding, gets the impression that Jessie still loves her ex-husband. This, plus mounting labor and other troubles at his plant which threaten to impoverish him, puts Hennessey temporarily on his uppers, morale-wise. But Jessie soon makes it apparent that her heart is now with Hennessey, that she will stick with him through his business troubles, and that the future is something they will face together.

What the critics said about MANNEQUIN

Frank Nugent in the New York Times

A glib, implausible, and smartly gowned little drama, as typically Metro-Goldwyn-Mayer as Leo himself, *Mannequin*, at the Capitol, restores Miss Joan Crawford to her throne as queen of the working girls, and reaffirms Katharine Brush's faith in the capitalist system. . . . Miss Crawford, let it be said, meets these several dramatic emergencies in her best manner, which, as you know, is tender, strong, heroic, and regal. For a Hester Street alumnus, she has a Park Avenue way about her, not to mention perfect diction and a curious remoteness from the odor of frankfurters and sauerkraut. . . . A slick restatement of an old theme, graced by a superior cast and directed with general skill by Frank Borzage, who has a gift for sentiment. All this is more than the story deserved, but about what one expects from an MGM *Mannequin* with Joan Crawford. Call it fair.

Howard Barnes in the New York Herald Tribune

Joan Crawford is not particularly happy in the role of the slum princess. Try as she may, she is too tony for Hester Street and too much Miss Crawford for the poor girl who made good. . . . *Mannequin* has good direction, acting and scenic investiture. All it lacks is a good story. It's a considerable lack.

With Spencer Tracy, Alan Curtis

With Spencer Tracy

The Shining Hour

A Metro-Goldwyn-Mayer Picture

(1938)

CAST: Joan Crawford, Margaret Sullavan, Robert Young, Melvyn Douglas, Fay Bainter, Allyn Joslyn, Hattie McDaniel, Oscar O'Shea, Frank Albertson, Harry Barris.

CREDITS: Based on the play by Keith Winter. Screenplay by Jane Murfin and Ogden Nash. Produced by Joseph L. Mankiewicz. Directed by Frank Borzage. Cameraman, George Folsey. Music, Franz Waxman. Dance arranged by De Marco. Costumes by Adrian. Editor, Frank E. Hull. Running time, 76 minutes.

SYNOPSIS

New York night-club dancer Olivia Riley (Joan Crawford) is courted by gentleman-farmer Henry Linden (Melvyn Douglas), who marries her despite the objections of his brother David (Robert Young). Olivia and Henry go to the family home, where Henry's and David's domineering sister Hannah Linden (Fay Bainter) presides. Hannah and Olivia do not hit it off, but Olivia likes David's wife Judy (Margaret Sullavan), who makes her feel welcome. David, it develops, has had very mixed feelings about Olivia from the beginning, and soon makes it apparent that he is attracted to her. She gradually reciprocates. Hannah senses the developing situation and tries to exploit it against Olivia, whom she wishes to discredit and drive away. Henry continues to be oblivious of his wife's growing involvement with David, but Judy realizes what is happening, and being a self-sacrificing, kindly type decides to put David's happiness above her own, if need be, and step aside. David is racked with guilt over his triangular dilemma, but the issue is not resolved until Hannah, in a fit of frustrated rage, sets fire to the house. Olivia rescues Judy in the nick of time, but Judy is badly burned. David goes up to Judy's bedroom where she is lying with her head swathed in bandages, only her expressive eyes showing. He realizes then that he has loved Judy all along, and he asks her forgiveness. Despite all Hannah's meddling, Olivia and Henry find that their relationship has not been permanently shattered, and decide to make a fresh start.

What one critic said about
THE SHINING HOUR

In Variety

The Shining Hour is studded with a quintet of marquee names, headed by Joan Crawford, but that draw value is all that exhibitors can depend on, as picture is a confused jungle of cross-purpose motivations and situations that fail entirely to arouse interest. Basic trouble with the production lies in confusing script. Frank Borzage could not overcome basic story faults in his direction. Production quality cannot be discounted but more is required to fill seats these days than eye-appealing sets and backgrounds.

With Melvyn Douglas, Fay Bainter, Margaret Sullavan, and Robert Young

With Melvyn Douglas

With Robert Young

The Ice Follies of 1939

A Metro-Goldwyn-Mayer Picture

(1939)

CAST: Joan Crawford, James Stewart, Lew Ayres, Lewis Stone, Bess Ehrhardt, Lionel Stander, Charles D. Brown. And "The International Ice Follies," with Bess Ehrhardt, Roy Shipstad, Eddie Shipstad, and Oscar Johnson.

CREDITS: From the story by Leonard Praskins. Screenplay by Florence Ryerson and Edgar Allan Woolf. Produced by Harry Rapf. Directed by Reinhold Schunzel. Cameramen, Joseph Ruttenberg, Oliver T. Marsh. Music, Roger Edens. Costumes by Adrian. Editor, W. Donn Hayes. Running time, 82 minutes.

SYNOPSIS

Mary McKay (Joan Crawford) is an aspiring actress in love with Larry Hall (James Stewart), an ice skater and would-be manager of ice shows. Larry does an act with Eddie Burgess (Lew Ayres), and all three pal around together. Though they are having financial difficulties, Mary and Larry are very much in love and want to marry. After the wedding, Larry has rough sledding when it comes to obtaining skating engagements, and Mary, speeding up her career ambitions in order to help out, finally succeeds in obtaining a stock contract with a film studio. On the lot she is "discovered" and becomes a star in her first film. Larry then goes East to generate interest in, and backing for, his Ice Follies idea. His plans go over and the Ice Follies is produced in New York, but Larry and Mary find themselves increasingly separated, first geographically, and then emotionally, by the demands of their respective careers. When Mary is sent East by studio head Douglas Tolliver, Jr. (Lewis Stone) for a personal appearance tour, she barely has time to see her husband, who is based in New York

with his show. Still, they have not stopped loving each other, and when Mary finally comes to realize that career ambitions are threatening to permanently destroy what she and Larry have between them, she tells Tolliver that her marriage means more to her than stardom, and asks for a release from her contract. But Tolliver solves the dilemma by hiring Larry to produce films, and the two happily return to Hollywood, their marriage saved and their love reinforced.

NOTE: Much of the footage for this film involved various numbers and turns done by "The International Ice Follies" with Bess Ehrhardt, Roy Shipstad, Eddie Shipstad, and Oscar Johnson.

What the critics said about THE ICE FOLLIES OF 1939

R. W. D. in the New York Herald Tribune

Since some kind of story was needed to lead up to the film debut of "The International Ice Follies," and top-flight players to give it the necessary publicity gloss, Joan Crawford, James Stewart, and Lew Ayres were given the unenviable job of trying to make it digestible. Their acting is smart and likeable; their material is not. . . . Little pretense is made to disguise the fact that the skating sequences at the end of the film were the reason for the production. . . . Miss Crawford should avoid this type of film in the future, when she has to buck poor material, a group of specialists and Metro's own lavishness. . . . the *Ice Follies of 1939* (second half) is a beautifully staged spectacle. The first half belongs in the cinema's Cain's warehouse.

B. R. C. in the New York Times

Miss Crawford, Mr. Stewart, Lew Ayres, Mr. Stone, and the others do as well as could be expected with such roles, the ice skating is nice, and the first picture Mr. Stewart produces is all in Technicolor.

With James Stewart and Lew Ayres

With Lewis Stone

The Women

A Metro-Goldwyn-Mayer Picture

(1939)

CAST: Norma Shearer, Joan Crawford, Rosalind Russell, Mary Boland, Paulette Goddard, Phyllis Povah, Joan Fontaine, Virginia Weidler, Lucile Watson, Florence Nash, Muriel Hutchinson, Esther Dale, Ann Moriss, Ruth Hussey, Dennie Moore, Mary Cecil, Mary Beth Hughes, Virginia Grey, Marjorie Main, Cora Witherspoon, Hedda Hopper.

CREDITS: Based on the play by Clare Boothe. Screenplay by Anita Loos and Jane Murfin. Produced by Hunt Stromberg. Directed by George Cukor. Cameramen, Oliver T. Marsh, Joseph Ruttenberg. Art Director, Cedric Gibbons. Music, Edward Ward, David Snell. Costumes by Adrian. Editor, Robert J. Kerns. Running time, 134 minutes.

SYNOPSIS

Mary Haines (Norma Shearer) is the warm, womanly, essentially kind-hearted wife of Stephen Haines (who does not appear in the film, nor does any other male). She is the loving and attentive mother of Little Mary (Virginia Weidler), and is altogether an admirable person who does unto others as she expects them to do unto her. Mary, however, is surrounded by a witchy social set, including Sylvia Fowler (Rosalind Russell), a gossipy man-trap; the Countess de Lave (Mary Boland), who has forgotten more about men than the rest of her friends will ever know; Miriam Aarons (Paulette Goddard), a hard-as-nails adventuress; plus assorted types cut from the same cloth. The "Witches' Congress" knows something that Mary doesn't know: that Stephen is having a surreptitious affair with Crystal Allen (Joan Crawford), an ambitious shopgirl. They see to it that Mary eventually learns of the existence of her rival and she and Crystal have it out in a gown-fitting room at a dress establishment, with the witches trying to listen in. Mary then makes the mistake of filing for divorce, and takes off for a Reno dude ranch with Sylvia, the Countess, and others who are likewise in the process of shedding their men. When the divorce is final, Stephen grieves Mary by marrying Crystal. Mary resigns herself to a lonely future, but when she hears (again through the grapevine) that Crystal is running true to form and has begun two-timing and otherwise mistreating Stephen, she puts on her new nail polish ("Jungle Red!") and goes out to do battle with Crystal. For once, Mary decides to play the love game the way the witches play it, and succeeds eminently. At the fadeout, having outplayed and outmaneuvered Crystal, Mary runs to meet the now contrite and conciliatory Stephen, and when one of her friends demurs, citing the necessity of pride in such a case, Mary answers with the classic line, "Pride is a luxury that a woman in love can't afford!"

What the critics said about THE WOMEN

In the New York Herald Tribune

Clare Boothe's vitriolic comedy on a segment of her sex . . . has been made into sure-fire screen entertainment. Some of the venom of the play has been extracted, while Miss Boothe's sentimental consideration of her heroine has become even more sentimental. What will matter to most film-goers is the fact that the show is caustically comic, that it has enlisted a slew of Hollywood's top actresses in its company, and that George Cukor, the atmosphere expert of the screen, has saturated the proceedings in femininity. Once more, *The Women* is a women's show, but one which is certain to flatter and amuse most men. . . . Joan Crawford gives a conventional but striking performance as the shopgirl who tries to hook the heroine's husband.

Frank Nugent in the New York Times

Miss Crawford is hard as nails in the Crystal Allen role, which is as it should be.

With Norma Shearer and Rosalind Russe

With unidentified player and Norma Shearer

With Phyllis Povah, Paulette Goddard, Rosalind Russell, Mary Boland, and Norma Shearer

With Clark Gable

Strange Cargo

A Metro-Goldwyn-Mayer Picture

(1940)

CAST: Joan Crawford, Clark Gable, Ian Hunter, Peter Lorre, Paul Lukas, Albert Dekker, J. Edward Bromberg, Eduardo Ciannelli, John Arledge, Frederic Worlock, Bernard Nedell, Victor Varconi.

CREDITS: Based on the book "Not Too Narrow, Not Too Deep" by Richard Sale. Screenplay by Lawrence Hazard. Produced by Joseph L. Mankiewicz. Directed by Frank Borzage. Cameraman, Robert Planck. Art Director, Cedric Gibbons. Music by Franz Waxman. Editor, Robert J. Kern. Running time, 113 minutes.

SYNOPSIS

Julie (Joan Crawford) is a café entertainer in a town near a French penal colony. Verne (Clark Gable), a prisoner, meets her while he is on wharf duty. Verne escapes and goes to her dressing room one night, but he is apprehended by the guards, and the café proprietor fires Julie for associating with a prisoner. At the prison, Moll (Albert Dekker) has engineered a jailbreak; he takes with him Cambreau (Ian Hunter), a gentle, mysterious, Christlike person; Telez (Eduardo Cianelli); Hessler (Paul Lukas); Dufond (John Arledge); and Flaubert (J. Edward Bromberg); also M'sieu Pig (Peter Lorre). Verne also escapes and taking Julie, he joins in with the other fugitives. The Christlike Cambreau exerts a spiritual influence over the other men, most of whom are criminals of the lowest order. Telez is the first to die, from snake bite, and he is given spiritual consolation by Cambreau at the end. As the group moves through the steaming jungle, finally taking refuge in an open boat on the ocean, others, including Dufond and Flaubert, die, having first been consoled by Cambreau. Moll, the toughest of the prisoners, is also favorably influenced by Cambreau. Finally, the only survivors are Julie, Verne, and Cambreau. For a time, the hardened and cynical, but basically decent, Verne scoffs at Cambreau's spiritual aura, but after pushing him overboard from their boat, then rescuing him, Verne begins to mend his ways. Finally, Verne determines to go back to finish his sentence, and Julie, who had hoped and prayed that Verne, whom she now loves, would also succumb to Cambreau's beneficent influence, promises to wait for him.

What the critics said about
STRANGE CARGO

In Film Daily

Here is a good, raw, stark melodrama which holds suspense from the start. Frank Borzage has given it expert directorial attention, with Joseph L. Mankiewicz filling the duties of producer. Clark Gable fits his role admirably, while Ian Hunter has never done better work. The acting is high-grade with Joan Crawford giving her best performance to date.

In Variety

Miss Crawford is provided with a particularly meaty role as the hardened dance-hall gal who falls hard for the tough convict. Role is a departure from those handed her during past several years by her studio, and reminiscent of her earlier work that carried her to popularity originally. Although the picture has its many deficiencies, the Crawford characterization will give studio execs idea of proper casting of her talents for the future. Direction by Frank Borzage fails to hit the dramatic punches. His seems to be a delayed delivery that disappoints on the whole. He has not clearly defined the spiritual redemption angle, which also adds to the audience confusion. The screenplay does not help Borzage out of his predicament.

With Ian Hunter and Clark Gable

Susan and God

A Metro-Goldwyn-Mayer Picture

(1940)

CAST: Joan Crawford, Fredric March, Ruth Hussey, John Carroll, Rita Hayworth, Nigel Bruce, Bruce Cabot, Rita Quigley, Rose Hobart, Constance Collier, Gloria DeHaven, Richard O. Crane, Norman Mitchell, Marjorie Main.

CREDITS: Based on the play by Rachel Crothers. Screenplay by Anita Loos. Produced by Hunt Stromberg. Directed by George Cukor. Cameraman, Robert Planck. Art Director, Cedric Gibbons. Music by Herbert Stothart. Costumes by Adrian. Editor, William H. Terhune. Running time, 117 minutes.

SYNOPSIS

Susan (Joan Crawford), a flighty and silly society matron, comes back from Europe all agog over a new religious thought movement that involves a public confession of all one's shortcomings. Aflame with the spirit of do-goodism, she tries to convert her jaded society friends to her new religious outlook, but most of them are too world-weary to show any enthusiasm. Susan's stupid meddling, however, does cause misunderstandings among such friends as "Hutchie" (Nigel Bruce) and his wife Charlotte (Ruth Hussey), and there is much resentment of her shallow priggishness. But Susan has been failing to practice what she preaches; her own domestic affairs are in sad disarray. She has been estranged from her intelligent and sensitive husband, Barrie (Fredric March), who has turned to drink because he finds his wife's selfishness and obtuseness unbearable. Susan also neglects her introverted, maladjusted daughter, Blossom (Rita Quigley), who has no self-confidence because of her mother's preoccupation with other matters. Barrie at first is taken in by Susan's new "religious" outlook, hoping it is a sign of growing maturity, but he soon comes to recognize it as just another manifestation of her shallow and insensitive nature. Barrie, for Blossom's sake, asks Susan to resume living with him, and she agrees, but without enthusiasm. Gradually, however, as Susan begins to perceive the emotional plight of her husband and child, she comes to realize that instead of meddling in other people's lives she ought to be putting her own in order; and when she realizes at last Barrie's and Blossom's genuine need of her, her finer womanly instincts are aroused, and she begins living the Golden Rule truly instead of preaching shallow variations of it.

What the critics said about
SUSAN AND GOD

In Variety

Joan Crawford provides a strong portrayal of Susan, a mature, matron characterization which is a marked departure for the player. There's still a tinge of the glamor girl in Miss Crawford but role provides the studio with key to future assignments for its star, which might bring her back considerably as a box-office personality. Picture indicates that Miss Crawford studiously followed the Gertrude Lawrence technique in the play in delivering the flighty and rapid-fire dialogue in the early sequences. . . . George Cukor's direction highlights the characterizations he unfolds.

Howard Barnes in the New York Herald Tribune

Since it is what is vaguely known as a woman's picture, the production ultimately depends on Miss Crawford's make-believe. While her characterization of Susan represents the best acting job she has done in a long time, she is not entirely successful in blending silliness with romantic power.

With Fredric March

With Rita Quigley and Fredric March

With Rita Quigley

With Bruce Cabot and Rose Hobart

With Rose Hobart

With Conrad Veidt

A Woman's Face

A Metro-Goldwyn-Mayer Picture

(1941)

CAST: Joan Crawford, Melvyn Douglas, Conrad Veidt, Osa Massen, Reginald Owen, Albert Bassermann, Marjorie Main, Donald Meek, Connie Gilchrist, Richard Nichols, Charles Quigley, Gwili Andre, Clifford Brooke, George Zucco, Henry Kolker, Robert Warwick, Gilbert Emery, Henry Daniell, Sarah Padden, William Farnum.

CREDITS: From the play "Il Etait Une Fois" by Francis de Croisset. Screenplay by Donald Ogden Stewart. Produced by Victor Saville. Directed by George Cukor. Cameraman, Robert Planck. Art Director, Cedric Gibbons. Music by Bronislau Kaper. Costumes by Adrian. Editor, Frank Sullivan. Running time, 105 minutes.

SYNOPSIS

Anna Holm (Joan Crawford) lives a lonely and embittered life in the gloomy Swedish capital, Stockholm. Scarred hideously on one side of her face by a childhood accident, she has turned to leading a ring of blackmailers as a reaction against a world that has shunned and scorned her. The ring she leads runs a roadhouse outside the capital, where she meets Torsten Barring (Conrad Veidt), a scheming and ambitious aristocrat who is financially embarrassed. Barring, sensing Anna's hunger for love and acceptance under her forbidding, defensive exterior, flatters and charms her.

Soon she is in love with him. Barring plans to use her in a diabolical plot to murder his young nephew, Lars-Erik (Richard Nichols), who stands between Torsten and the fortune of his aging father, Consul Magnus Barring (Albert Bassermann). Meanwhile, Anna deludes herself that Barring cares as deeply for her as she does for him. Vera Segert (Osa Massen), wife of Dr. Gustav Segert (Melvyn Douglas), a plastic surgeon, is a frivolous, philandering little baggage who has written indiscreet love letters which come into Anna's possession. Anna goes to Vera's house with the letters, seeking blackmail, and is forced to hide when Dr. Segert returns unexpectedly. Surprised by the doctor in his consulting room, Anna sprains an ankle attempting to escape. Vera pretends Anna is an intruder, but begs the doctor to let her go. Dr. Segert notices Anna's scarred face and his healing instincts take over. He suggests to her an operation which is risky but if successful will leave her as normal in appearance as anyone. Anna agrees to the operation, which *is* successful. She is now a strikingly beautiful young woman. Gustav, who realizes that he has healed only the surface, not the interior distortions, wonders aloud if he has created a Galatea or a Frankenstein monster. Anna goes immediately to the apartment of Torsten, with whom she is still in love, and surprises him with her new appearance. Torsten persuades her to go along with his plan to murder his nephew. He inveigles Anna into his father's household as Lars-Erik's governess. Gradually Anna becomes attached to the boy, and

With Osa Massen

With Melvyn Douglas

With Albert Bassermann, Marjorie Main, and Richard Nichols

when the time comes to carry out the murder plan
—which involves the unlatching of the safety-
catch of a cable car running over a mountain
pass, from which the boy is "accidentally" to fall
—Anna finds she is unable to do it. Gustav, who
also happens to be a visitor at the Barring country
place, has become suspicious of the goings-on, and
watches the cable-car incident through field
glasses. Torsten, infuriated by Anna's failure to
follow through, and realizing that she has ceased
to love him and has had a spiritual rebirth, attempts to kill the boy himself during an evening's
sleighing party. But Anna shoots him and saves
the child. At the subsequent murder trial Anna is
exonerated when a letter is discovered in which
she tried to warn the Consul against Torsten's
machinations. Gustav and Anna discover that they
are in love.

What one critic said about
A WOMAN'S FACE
In Variety

Miss Crawford takes a radical step as a screen
glamour girl to allow the makeup necessary for
facial disfiguration in the first half; an innova-
tion that might well interest other screen stars
with dramatic tendencies to be receptive to similar roles that may require temporary or permanent marring of facial beauty. . . . Miss Crawford
has a strongly dramatic and sympathetic role . . .
which she handles in top-notch fashion.

With Conrad Veidt

With Connie Gilchrist, Donald Meek, and Reginald Owen

144

When Ladies Meet

A Metro-Goldwyn-Mayer Picture

(1941)

CAST: Joan Crawford, Robert Taylor, Greer Garson, Herbert Marshall, Spring Byington, Rafael Strom, Florence Shirley, Leslie Francis, Olaf Hytten, Mona Barrie.

CREDITS: Based on the play by Rachel Crothers. Screenplay by S. K. Lauren and Anita Loos. Produced by Robert Z. Leonard and Orville O. Dull. Directed by Robert Z. Leonard. Cameraman, Robert Planck. Art Director, Cedric Gibbons. Music by Bronislau Kaper. Costumes by Adrian. Editor, Robert Kern. Running time, 105 minutes.

SYNOPSIS

Mary Howard (Joan Crawford) is a successful novelist with "advanced" ideas about love and marriage. In love with her publisher, Rogers Woodruff (Herbert Marshall), who happens to be married, Mary is pursued by Jimmy Lee (Robert Taylor), who is convinced that he, not Rogers, is the right man for her. He does, however, have difficulty in convincing Mary of this. Meanwhile, Mary tolerates Jimmy for laughs while taking very seriously herself, her career, and her affair with Woodruff. Adopting an analytical, objective approach to her temporary "back street" status, Mary decides that taking Rogers away from his wife and getting him to marry her is the only logical, civilized thing to do. Jimmy, who sees through her rationalizations and general wrong-thinking, decides to throw her together with Rogers' wife, Clare (Greer Garson), at the home of a friend, Bridget Drake (Spring Byington). Neither Clare nor Mary know each other, or their respective relationships to Rogers. Both stay overnight at Bridget's, take a liking to each other, and have a long woman-to-woman before-bed chat, during which Mary is deeply affected by Clare's womanly maturity and mellow charm. Mary learns from Clare that Rogers, whom she has passionately idolized, is actually a philandering fool of long standing, and that Clare, who loves him sincerely and realistically and has tolerated his womanizing for years, understands him and in her way respects him, as Mary finds she never could. Realizing that she no longer loves Rogers, Mary is ripe at last for patient, humorous Jimmy Lee's overtures—and he proceeds to make them. This time, Jimmy finds Mary more than receptive.

What the critics said about
WHEN LADIES MEET

Bosley Crowther in the New York Times

In this loquacious trifle, Joan Crawford plays the lady novelist with impressive but unaffecting intensity, robed in the most spectacular gowns.

With Herbert Marshall

Howard Barnes in the New York Herald Tribune
Joan Crawford . . . as the novelist, who tries to be very civilized about breaking up a marriage, fusses about her terrace apartment or postures in striking gowns, with little more to do than talk about true love or problems of writing. Even when she wears spectacles, she is not particularly convincing in the part.

With Greer Garson

With Greer Garson

With Robert Taylor

With Herbert Marshall

With Melvyn Douglas

They All Kissed the Bride

A Columbia Picture

(1942)

CAST: Joan Crawford, Melvyn Douglas, Roland Young, Billie Burke, Andrew Tombes, Allen Jenkins, Helen Parrish, Emory Parnell, Mary Treen, Nydia Westman, Ivan Simpson, Roger Clark, Gordon Jones, Edward Gargan.

CREDITS: From the story by Gina Kaus and Andrew P. Solt. Screenplay by P. J. Wolfson. Produced by Edward Kaufman. Directed by Alexander Hall. Cameraman, Joseph Walker. Art Directors, Lionel Banks and Cary Odell. Music by M. Stoloff. Costumes by Irene. Editor, Viola Lawrence. Running time, 86 minutes.

SYNOPSIS

Margaret J. Drew (Joan Crawford) is a hard-nosed, shrewish, businesslike career woman with a maximum of will-to-power and a minimum of sense of humor. She is the elder daughter of a trucking magnate, and when her father dies she takes over the business. Margaret ruthlessly rides herd on everyone, including her mother, Mrs. Drew

(Billie Burke), a fluttery, ineffectual matron; her younger sister, Vivian (Helen Parrish), whom she is determined to force into an unromantic but socially and financially advantageous marriage; her hapless board of directors, who tremble before her icy efficiency and gusty rages; and the hundreds of truck drivers under her firm's command. Michael Holmes (Melvyn Douglas), a crusading, icon-smashing journalist, writes a series of articles that portray Margaret in all her power-struggles, and Margaret proceeds to do battle with him. Michael is attracted to her despite her mannish arrogance and brittle ways, and he decides to defrost the iron-icicle tycoon. Her urges her to look into the living habits of her truck drivers, and takes her to a company dance where she suddenly finds herself doing a frantic jitterbug with truck driver Johnny Johnson (Allen Jenkins). Michael has deliberately cultivated a friendship with the cooperatively talkative Johnson to get the goods on Margaret and her firm. Meanwhile, Margaret has Discovered Love, and is slowly defrosting under the hot rays of Michael's affectionate overtures and relaxing, ingratiating personality. She ceases firing employees at the slightest provocation, begins to

With Melvyn Douglas and unidentified player

With Roland Young

watch her appearance more, and mellows tolerantly in the face of the problems her relatives present. Margaret, in short, has learned to be a woman, and the prognosis for her and Michael's future together is positive.

What one critic said about
THEY ALL KISSED THE BRIDE

Robert W. Dana in the New York Herald Tribune
Joan Crawford's return to the screen is under such pleasant auspices, for she and Columbia's brilliant director Alexander Hall and the comedy-wise Melvyn Douglas make the most of a well-written, cleverly constructed screen story. . . . Not in many a day have we seen the risqué possibilities of romance and its biological allusions treated on the screen with such frankness and finesse. Miss Crawford demonstrates the range of her talent in those sequences which compel her to change the personality of her heroine gradually from that of a machinelike businesswoman to that of an awakened young beauty with a desire to be an expert jitterbug.

Reunion in France

A Metro-Goldwyn-Mayer Picture

(1942)

CAST: Joan Crawford, John Wayne, Philip Dorn, Reginald Owen, Albert Bassermann, John Carradine, Ann Ayars, J. Edward Bromberg, Moroni Olsen, Howard Da Silva, Henry Daniell.

CREDITS: Based on an original screen story by Ladislas Bus-Fekete. Screenplay, Jan Lustig, Marvin Borowsky, and Marc Connelly. Produced by Joseph L. Mankiewicz. Directed by Jules Dassin. Cameraman, Robert Planck. Art Director, Cedric Gibbons. Music, Franz Waxman. Costumes by Irene. Editor, Elmo Veron. Running time, 102 minutes.

SYNOPSIS

Michele de la Becque (Joan Crawford) is a giddy, spoiled, and well-heeled Parisian career woman. She takes nothing seriously, not even love. The coming of World War II hardly causes a ripple in her ordered world. She is in love with an industrial designer, Robert Cortot (Philip Dorn), and they conduct their lives amidst luxurious surroundings in the highest social circles, with the best happening in the best of all possible worlds. Gradually, the realities of war and collaboration in a defeated and prostrate France intrude on the even pace of her life. Inadvertently, Michele discovers that Robert is hobnobbing with Nazi officers and that his industrial plants are turning out weapons for the Nazis. Never much of a French patriot up till then, Michele finds herself outraged and disillusioned, and she confronts Robert stormily with the proof of his practices. Robert is evasive, noncommittal, does not deny her charges. A suddenly alerted Michele begins to take note at last of the disordered French world around her. Paris is gloomy, and a crippled France is compromising as best it can with the brutal realities of the Nazi occupation. Bewildered and unhappy, Michele goes to the aid of an American flier, Pat Talbot (John Wayne), who has been downed in French territory and is being hunted by the Gestapo. An affectionate attachment arises between them, but Michele is not at all sure of her feelings. Then she discovers, to her great joy and relief, that Robert is not a Nazi collaborator after all, that while he is turning out weapons for the Nazis he is making sure they are defective and, moreover, is organizing a secret French force that will strike out at France's oppressors when the time is ripe. Robert and Michele are happily reunited.

What the critics said about
REUNION IN FRANCE

In Film Daily

Miss Crawford, while she isn't always convincing as a Frenchwoman, does manage to give a good account of herself in the leading role. . . . The film, directed capably by Jules Dassin, has been given a first-rate production by Joseph L. Mankiewicz.

T. S. in the New York Times

Miss Crawford, as usual, makes an elegant mannequin for a series of ensembles that probably will excite more female comment than the role itself.

Joseph Pihodna in the New York Herald Tribune

Suffice to say that Miss Crawford appears in enough new dresses to please producers and the feminine audience. With all the evidence in, Miss Crawford, as Michele de la Becque, isn't making all the sacrifices implied in the script. She has certain prerogatives. Dressing like a refugee is certainly not in her contract.

With John Wayne and Philip Dorn

Above Suspicion

A Metro-Goldwyn-Mayer Picture

(1943)

CAST: Joan Crawford, Fred MacMurray, Conrad Veidt, Basil Rathbone, Reginald Owen, Cecil Cunningham, Richard Ainley, Ann Shoemaker, Sara Haden, Felix Bressart, Bruce Lestor, Johanna Hoper, Lotta Palfi, Alex Papana.

CREDITS: Based on the novel by Helen Mac-Innes. Screenplay by Keith Winter, Melville Baker, and Patricia Coleman. Produced by Victor Saville. Directed by Richard Thorpe. Cameraman, Robert Planck. Art, Randall Duell. Music by Bronislau Kaper. Costumes by Irene, Gile Steele. Running time, 91 minutes.

SYNOPSIS

Frances Myles (Joan Crawford) and her husband, Richard Myles (Fred MacMurray), are newlywed Americans visiting England just prior to the outbreak of World War II. They find themselves, through a series of contretemps, drafted by the British secret service for a strange mission to Germany, which they had planned to visit on their honeymoon anyway. They are commissioned to secure, through a series of secret agents, some vital confidential plans for a new secret weapon—a magnetic mine. First they go to Paris, from whence the trail leads to Salzburg, with agents, both allied and enemy, confronting them on many occasions, then disappearing as fast as they have come. In Salzburg, they attract the attention of the Gestapo chief, Sig Von Aschenhausen (Basil Rathbone), who spies constantly on their activities. In an attempt to get over the border, Frances and Richard assume disguises, but these fail and they are recognized. They obtain the information they were assigned to get, and the continuing problem remains: how to get out of the country with it. Then Frances is captured by the Gestapo and kept prisoner in a remote castle. She is rescued by Richard and a group of British agents, and following underground routes, they finally get across the border to safety.

What the critics said about ABOVE SUSPICION

Howard Barnes in the New York Herald Tribune

There are so many spies in *Above Suspicion* that it is hard to keep track of them. There are so many floral, musical, and cryptographical passwords in the film's plot that the whole show becomes a sort of super treasure hunt. . . . Unfortunately, neither Joan Crawford nor Fred MacMurray look quite bright enough to unravel the tangled skeins of this screen melodrama.

T. S. in the New York Times

Joan Crawford, after a couple of pretentious roles, is a very convincing heroine.

In Variety

Both MacMurray and Miss Crawford competently handled their roles, despite drawbacks of script material.

With Fred MacMurray and unidentified player

152

With Fred MacMurray and Conrad Veidt

With Fred MacMurray

With Fred MacMurray, Sara Haden, and Ann Shoemaker

With Fred MacMurray and unidentified players

154

Hollywood Canteen

A Warner Brothers Picture

(1944)

CAST: Joan Leslie, Robert Hutton, Dane Clark, Janis Paige. And, in alphabetical order, guest stars: the Andrews Sisters, Jack Benny, Joe E. Brown, Eddie Cantor, Kitty Carlisle, Jack Carson, Joan Crawford, Bette Davis, John Garfield, Sydney Greenstreet, Paul Henreid, Peter Lorre, Ida Lupino, Irene Manning, Joan McCracken, Dennis Morgan, Eleanor Parker, Roy Rogers and Trigger, Barbara Stanwyck, Jane Wyman.

CREDITS: Original screenplay by Delmer Daves. Produced by Alex Gottlieb. Directed by Delmer Daves. Cameraman, Bert Glennon. Art Director, Leo Kuter. Musical Director, Leo F. Forbstein. Musical numbers created by LeRoy Prinz. Music adapted by Ray Heindorf. Editor, Christian Nyby. Running time, 123 minutes.

SYNOPSIS

Two soldiers on sick leave spend three exciting nights at the famed Hollywood Canteen before returning to active duty in the Pacific. Slim (Robert Hutton) happens to be the millionth G.I. to enjoy the hospitality of the Canteen. Accordingly, he wins a date with Joan Leslie. The other G.I., Sergeant (Dane Clark), gets to dance with Joan Crawford. Canteen President Bette Davis and Vice President John Garfield give talks on the Canteen's history. The soldiers enjoy various musical numbers offered by such volunteer performers as Dennis Morgan, Joe E. Brown, the Golden Gate Quartet, Kitty Carlisle, Jane Wyman, Jack Carson, Eddie Cantor, Nora Martin, Roy Rogers, and Sons of the Pioneers. Also performing are Joseph Szigeti and Jack Benny (who do a violin duet), the Andrews Sisters, and Joan McCracken.

What the critics said about HOLLYWOOD CANTEEN

In Variety

There isn't a marquee big enough to hold all the names in this one, so how can it miss? Besides, it's basically solid. It has story, cohesion, and heart. That's not a bad parlay, either.

Kate Cameron in the New York Daily News

It is an elaborate show, but it is presented by author-director Delmer Daves in such a patronizing manner as to make one blush for its complete lack of reserve in singing the praises of Hollywood. It boasts screen personages unashamedly and without a flicker of humor. The players in the picture seem constantly awed by their own gracious and hospitable entertainment of the servicemen.

With Dane Clark

Mildred Pierce

A Warner Brothers Picture

(1945)

CAST: Joan Crawford, Jack Carson, Zachary Scott, Eve Arden, Ann Blyth, Bruce Bennett, George Tobias, Lee Patrick, Moroni Olsen, Jo Ann Marlow, Barbara Brown.

CREDITS: From the novel by James M. Cain. Screenplay by Ranald MacDougall. Produced by Jerry Wald. Directed by Michael Curtiz. Cameraman, Ernest Haller. Art Director, Anton Grot. Music by Max Steiner. Costumes by Milo Anderson. Editor, David Weisbart. Running time, 111 minutes.

SYNOPSIS

Mildred Pierce (Joan Crawford) is a restless, ambitious woman, mother of two half-grown daughters, who is dissatisfied with her financially lean marriage to Bert Pierce (Bruce Bennett) and has channeled all her devotion to her children, especially her older daughter, Veda (Ann Blyth). Veda is spoiled, demanding, and snobbish, and taunts Mildred with her humble origins. Mildred, blindly adoring, indulges Veda's whims, doing odd jobs to keep her in nice clothes. Bert, who feels shut out, has turned for consolation to another woman, Maggie Binderhof (Lee Patrick), and eventually he and Mildred reach a parting of the ways. Goaded on by Veda's insatiable demands, Mildred becomes ambitious, opens a small restaurant with the help of real estate man Wally Fay (Jack Carson). Wally is a blunt and vulgar type who is forever making passes, which Mildred rebuffs. Wally takes her to aristocratic Monte Beragon (Zachary Scott), who is on his uppers financially, and her earnestness charms Monte into giving her the use of one of his properties for the restaurant. The business prospers and develops into a chain. Veda, selfish and demanding as ever, takes up with Monte, who cares for Mildred in his rakish, weak way but realizes also that she has a permanent hang-up on Veda. Mildred, who at first imagines herself in love with Monte, becomes disenchanted with his profligate ways, orders him to leave Veda alone, and dismisses him with a substantial check. Veda gets money out of a wealthy family on the pretext that she is to have a baby by their son. Mildred, angered at Veda's lying, ruthless ways, tears up the $10,000 check in front of Veda, and Veda slaps her. Enraged, Mildred orders her out. Mildred travels, tries to forget about Veda but cannot. She goes to find her daughter, who is singing in a cheap joint. Veda indicates she would return home if Mildred could give her the luxurious life she craves. The now affluent Mildred makes a deal with Monte to marry him and take over his lavish but rundown home so as to provide the proper

With Zachary Scott

With Jack Carson

background for Veda. Monte insists on one-third of Mildred's business in return; she agrees. Veda and Monte begin carrying on behind Mildred's back. Monte sells out his one-third interest in Mildred's business, forcing her into bankruptcy. She then learns about him and Veda. Enraged, she goes to Monte's beach house, finds him with Veda. Monte takes a gun away from Mildred. She leaves, distraught. Outside in the car, she hears a shot. Veda, scorned by Monte, whom she wishes to marry, has murdered him. Mildred tries to protect her daughter by confessing to the murder, but the police gradually get the truth. At the end, Veda faces a prison term, and Mildred, it is inferred, will return to Bert whom, she now realizes, she had always neglected for her daughter.

What the critics said about
MILDRED PIERCE

Thomas M. Pryor in the New York Times

Joan Crawford is playing a most troubled lady, and giving a sincere and generally effective characterization of same, in the new drama of James M. Cain origin, *Mildred Pierce*. It is a tribute to Miss Crawford's art that Mildred comes through as well as she does.

Howard Barnes in the New York Herald Tribune

Miss Crawford is very intense and restrained in the title role. She plays with studied underemphasis a doting mother who spoils her monstrous daughter so badly that the latter tries to steal her second husband away from her.

With Ann Blyth and Zachary Scott

With Zachary Scott

With Zachary Scott and Jack Carson

Humoresque

A Warner Brothers Picture

(1946)

CAST: Joan Crawford, John Garfield, Oscar Levant, J. Carroll Naish, Joan Chandler, Tom D'Andrea, Peggy Knudsen, Ruth Nelson, Craig Stevens, Paul Cavanaugh, Richard Gaines, John Abbott, Bobby Blake, Tommy Cook, Don McGuire, Fritz Leiber, Peg La Centra, Nestor Paiva, Richard Walsh.

CREDITS: Based on a story by Fannie Hurst. Screenplay by Clifford Odets and Zachary Gold. Produced by Jerry Wald. Directed by Jean Negulesco. Cameraman, Ernest Haller. Art Director, Hugh Reticker. Music conducted by Franz Waxman. Musical Director, Leo F. Forbstein. Music Advisor, Isaac Stern. Miss Crawford's costumes by Adrian. Editor, Rudi Fehr. Running time, 125 minutes.

SYNOPSIS

Ambitious, temperamental, and independent young violinist Paul Boray (John Garfield) plays at a party given by neurotic, dissolute Helen Wright (Joan Crawford), a wealthy dilettante. She is bogged down in a loveless marriage with aging Victor Wright (Paul Cavanaugh), who understands, and is tolerant of, Helen's vagaries and assorted infidelities. Nymphomaniacal and self-centered, Helen uses men as sexual toys. Paul baffles her; she has never before encountered, at close range, a dedicated artist who refuses to be owned or dominated. Shortly, she is in love with him but fights her feelings, knowing that her undisciplined, sybaritic past can only taint his future. Also, she is essentially afraid of love, feeling unable to cope with it because of her unfortunate past conditionings. Meanwhile, she fosters Paul's career, introduces him to a prominent musical impresario, and helps him to success. Paul returns her love, but finds her nature too complex for him to handle. Paul's mother disapproves of his involvement with the married Helen, and when Helen goes to see her, hoping for some kind of elucidation and purgation of her tragic dilemma, the mother coldly advises that they separate. Helen and Paul quarrel. She encounters him with an earlier girl friend, and is unreasoningly jealous. Finally, hit with the full awareness that, despite their love for each other, they are hopelessly unsuited for any future together, Helen realizes bitterly that this is only the latest of her always destructive relationships. Helen de-

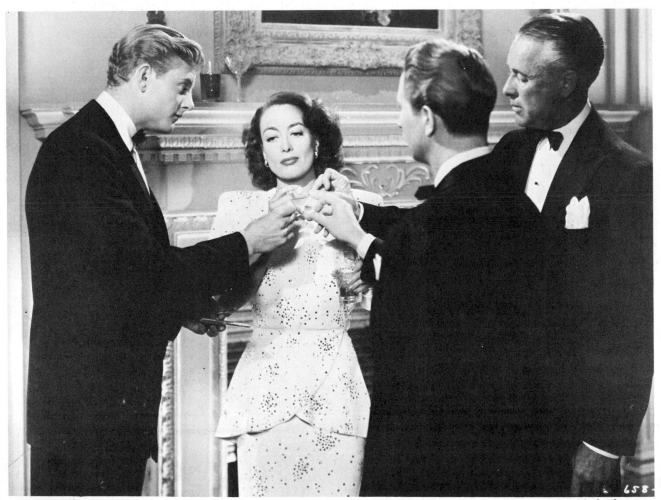

With John Garfield

With unidentified players

With John Garfield

With Craig Stevens and Paul Cavanaugh

cides not to attend a concert at which Paul, who still loves her and hopes for a solution to their problem, is playing Wagner's *Liebestod.* . Helen listens to it on the radio, then walks into the nearby ocean. She has resolved their dilemma in the only way logical to her jaded, tormented nature.

What the critics said about HUMORESQUE

Lawrence J. Quirk in Screen Stars (Retrospective Review)

Humoresque is undoubtedly Crawford's finest performance (*Possessed* runs a close second). I have seen this film a number of times, and I suspect that Crawford attained an extra dimension of romantic lyricism and dramatic sincerity in this because it was made at the time she received her Oscar for *Mildred Pierce*, and, for the first time truly confident of her powers, and inwardly fortified by the acclamation of her peers, she strode through the role with a grand self-confidence and a sweeping grasp of the part's emotional possibilities. As Helen, the dissolute and wealthy patroness of a fast-rising violinist, played by John Garfield, she was forceful, suitably complex, aglow with feeling. Her timing was flawless, her appearance lovely, her emotions depthful. Her love scenes with Garfield carried ultimate conviction, and in one scene, in which she sits in a box reliving the feelings Garfield is re-creating with his violin on the concert stage, the cameraman, in a series of stunning close-up shots does full justice to her graphic facial renditions of deeply felt emotion. A glamorous role for Crawford, a glamorous picture, and its like is not to be seen today.

With Paul Cavanaugh and John Garfield

Possessed

A Warner Brothers Picture

(1947)

CAST: Joan Crawford, Van Heflin, Raymond Massey, Geraldine Brooks, Stanley Ridges, John Ridgely, Moroni Olsen; Erskine Sanford, Gerald Perreau, Isabel Withers, Lisa Golm, Douglas Kennedy, Monte Blue, Don McGuire, Rory Mallinson, Clifton Young, Griff Barnett.

CREDITS: Based on the story "One Man's Secret!" by Rita Weiman. Screenplay by Silvia Richards and Ranald MacDougall. Produced by Jerry Wald. Directed by Curtis Bernhardt. Cameraman, Joseph Valentine. Art Director, Anton Grot. Music by Franz Waxman. Miss Crawford's costumes by Adrian. Editor, Rudi Fehr. Running time, 108 minutes.

SYNOPSIS

Louise Howell (Joan Crawford) is an emotionally unstable young woman working as a nurse for the invalid wife of wealthy Dean Graham (Raymond Massey). She is in love with engineer David Sutton (Van Heflin); however, she loves not wisely but too well. David, disgusted and alienated by Louise's possessive, smothering, somewhat maniacal obsession for him, informs her that he does not return her feeling and wishes to break off. Whereupon she threatens him. He leaves her then without a word. Meanwhile Dean's invalid wife, a querulous, demanding woman, keeps insisting that her husband is having an affair with Louise. This, of course, is purely the product of her overwrought imagination; she drowns herself shortly thereafter. Louise remains on as Dean's housekeeper and cares for his younger child, Wynn (Gerald Perreau). Dean's daughter, Carol (Geraldine Brooks), at first believes the letters her mother had written her about Louise and Dean and keeps her distance, sulking at boarding school. David reenters the scene, having taken an engineering job with Dean, and Louise, having learned nothing from experience, again pursues him. David repulses her sarcastically. Dean asks Louise to marry him, and in desperation she agrees, seeking to salve her wounded self-image. Louise wins over Carol by offering not to marry Dean if Carol disapproves. After the marriage, David persists in hanging around and begins courting Carol, who is innocent of her stepmother's obsession for him. Taunted by David, who has lost respect for her because of her emotional excesses, Louise's overwrought, hysterical mind starts to crumble. She begins hearing imagi-

nary noises; reality and unreality become hazy in her mind; she imagines that her husband's first wife is still alive. Frantically she tries to break up the forthcoming marriage of David and Carol, and when her attempt fails she goes to David's apartment and shoots and kills him in an all-out burst of homicidal madness. Then she flees the city and is later found in Los Angeles, wandering around in a pitiful mental state. Brought to a hospital she is diagnosed as psychotic. The attending psychiatrist (Stanley Ridges) tells the sorrowing Dean that Louise was neither mentally nor morally responsible for her actions when she killed David. The prognosis: much mental suffering for Louise, a possible cure eventually. It is indicated that the faithful, long-suffering Dean will stand by.

What the critics said about POSSESSED

James Agee in Time

Most of it is filmed with unusual imaginativeness and force. The film is uncommonly well acted. Miss Crawford is generally excellent, performing with the passion and intelligence of an actress who is not content with just one Oscar. In fact, the weaknesses in this unusual movie do not greatly matter beside the fact that a lot of people who have a lot to give are giving it all they've got.

Howard Barnes in the New York Herald Tribune

Miss Crawford is at her best in the mad scenes. The actress has obviously studied the aspects of insanity to re-create a rather terrifying portrait of a woman possessed by devils.

With Van Heflin

With Van Heflin

With Van Heflin

Daisy Kenyon

A 20th Century-Fox Picture

(1947)

CAST: Joan Crawford, Dana Andrews, Henry Fonda, Ruth Warrick, Martha Stewart, Peggy Ann Garner, Connie Marshall, Nicholas Joy, Art Baker, Robert Karnes, John Davidson, Victoria Horne, Charles Meredith, Roy Roberts, Griff Barnett.

CREDITS: From the novel by Elizabeth Janeway. Screenplay by David Hertz. Produced and directed by Otto Preminger. Cameraman, Leon Shamroy. Art Directors, Lyle Wheeler and George Davis. Musical score, David Raskin. Musical Director, Alfred Newman. Costumes by Charles Le-Maire. Editor, Louis Loeffler. Running time, 99 minutes.

SYNOPSIS

Daisy Kenyon (Joan Crawford) is a commercial artist who lives in Greenwich Village and has been forced into an uneasy "back street" relationship with high-powered lawyer Dan O'Mara (Dana Andrews), who is married and a father. Daisy isn't happy with the status quo; she wants Dan to choose between his wife Lucille (Ruth Warrick) and her. Because she is deeply in love with the self-centered Dan, Daisy reluctantly continues the arrangement, accepting whatever crumbs of his time Dan can give her. Enter Peter (Henry Fonda), who offers Daisy a complete and untrammeled relationship. Daisy decides it's better to be loved than to love, and marries Peter. Meanwhile, Dan's wife overhears a phone conversation between Dan and Daisy, and breaks in on it hysterically. Dan, fed up with the wife he has ceased to love, gets a divorce at last. He then tries to pressure the now married Daisy into returning to him. Peter decides to take an objective, psychological approach to the situation, and leaves the choice up to Daisy. Daisy realizes she has stopped loving Dan and remains with Peter, whose quiet self-confidence and stable temperament have at last won her over.

What the critics said about DAISY KENYON

T. M. P. in the New York Times

Joan Crawford is having man-trouble again. . . . Miss Crawford is, of course, an old hand at being an emotionally confused and frustrated woman, and she plays the role with easy competence.

Otis L. Guernsey, Jr. in the New York Herald Tribune

Preminger accomplishes no mean feat in guiding these people in and out among the interweavings of their own complexes, and he does wonders in varying the action of similar scenes. Working with Miss Crawford's iridescence, Fonda's diffidence, and Andrews' aggressiveness, he stages these synthetic involvements as though he believed every minute of them.

With Henry Fonda

With Dana Andrews

With Dana Andrews and Henry Fonda

Flamingo Road

A Warner Brothers Picture
(1949)

CAST: Joan Crawford, Zachary Scott, Sydney Greenstreet, Gladys George, Virginia Huston, Fred Clark, Gertrude Michael, Alice White, Sam McDaniel, Tito Vuolo, David Brian.

CREDITS: From the play by Robert and Sally Wilder. Screenplay by Robert Wilder. Producer, Jerry Wald. Directed by Michael Curtiz. Cameraman, Ted McCord. Art Director, Leo K. Kuter. Musical score, Max Steiner. Musical Director, Ray Heindorf. Miss Crawford's costumes designed by Travilla, executed by Sheila O'Brien. Editor, Folmar Blangsted. Running time, 96 minutes.

SYNOPSIS

Lane Bellamy (Joan Crawford), a carnival dancer, finds herself stranded in a small Southern town bossed by Titus Semple (Sidney Greenstreet), whose deputy is charming but weak Fielding Carlisle (Zachary Scott). Lane and Fielding are attracted to each other, and he helps her get a waitress job. Semple has political ambitions for his deputy and considers Lane an inappropriate match for him. When Semple gets Lane fired, she confronts him defiantly and Semple frames her on a prostitution rap. Then Semple pushes Fielding into marriage with socialite Annabelle Weldon (Virginia Huston). After some months in prison, the enterprising and forthright Lane returns to the town, intent on revenge. She gets a job in a roadhouse run by Lute·Mae Sanders (Gladys George), who provides feminine companionship for the area's influential men. One of Lute Mae's patrons is a rising political mover-

With two unidentified dancers

and-shaker named Dan Reynolds (David Brian), and he and Lane begin dating. Reynolds does not get along with Semple, and he is locked with Lane's old enemy in a power-struggle. Lane is still in love with Fielding but agrees to marry Reynolds, and together they climb to the top. When Lane, who now realizes that she loves her husband, is given reason to believe that Semple is out to ruin him totally, she is enraged. Fielding, who has been fired by Semple, comes to Lane's house and kills himself. There is a scandal, which Semple exploits. Lane goes to see Semple, they quarrel, struggle for the gun that Lane had impulsively taken along, and Lane kills Semple accidentally. At the end there is a note of hope as Lane waits in prison for a ruling and Dan appears and indicates that he will stick by her.

What one critic said about

FLAMINGO ROAD

Howard Barnes in the New York Herald Tribune
Joan Crawford acquits herself ably in an utterly nonsensical and undefined part. As a carnival performer who determines to move to the right side of an anomalous town, she is attractive and vital. It is no fault of hers that she cannot handle the complicated romances and double crosses in which she is involved. Maintaining an impeccable reputation by virtue of Hollywood's tacit censorship, she falls in love with one man, marries another, and finally kills the villain. The recurrent line in her dialogue is: "I'm not sure."

It's a Great Feeling

A Warner Brothers Picture

(1949)

CAST: Dennis Morgan, Doris Day, Jack Carson, Bill Goodwin, Irving Bacon, Claire Carleton, Harlan Warde, Jacqueline de Wit. Guest appearances by: Gary Cooper, Edward G. Robinson, Joan Crawford, Danny Kaye, Errol Flynn, Ronald Reagan, Jane Wyman, Eleanor Parker, Patricia Neal.

CREDITS: From a story by I. A. L. Diamond. Screenplay by Jack Rose and Mel Shavelson. Produced by Alex Gottlieb. Directed by David Butler. Cameraman, Wilfrid M. Cline. Art Director, Stanley Fleischer. Music by Ray Heindorf. Editor, Irene Morra. Running time, 85 minutes.

SYNOPSIS

A broad takeoff on picture-making and Hollywood customs in general, the story centers around Jack Carson's efforts to direct himself and Dennis Morgan (both playing themselves) in a film produced by harassed Arthur Trent (Bill Goodwin). Carson's directorial arrangement is a stop-gap, last-resort move by Trent, because none of the top directors at Warners want to work with Carson. The directors, under their own names, make brief appearances at this point in the film, and include: Michael Curtiz, King Vidor, David Butler, and Raoul Walsh. Doris Day plays Judy Adams, a studio restaurant waitress who wants to crack films; she is discovered by Carson and Morgan and starred in the film they are making. Guest stars who are worked naturally into the action include Gary Cooper, Ronald Reagan, Edward G. Robinson, Jane Wyman, Danny Kaye, Errol Flynn, Eleanor Parker, and Patricia Neal. Joan Crawford appears in a gown shop sequence with Carson and Morgan, and does a hilarious spoof of her usual sophisticated screen personality. Among the songs offered are: Doris Day and Dennis Morgan singing "Blame My Absent-minded Heart," Doris singing "At the Café Rendezvous," Doris and Jack Carson singing "That Was a Big Fat Lie," and Dennis, Jack, and Doris singing "There's Nothing Rougher Than Love."

What the critics said about IT'S A GREAT FEELING

Joe Pihodna in the New York Herald Tribune

Joan Crawford proves to be an amazingly deft comedienne. . . .

A. H. Weiler in the New York Times

Joan Crawford spoofs her own woman-of-the-world roles.

In Variety

Joan Crawford does a pip of a bit in a swank gown shop with the three principals, rating plenty of howls. . . . The guests are brought into the story naturally and this lack of forced use is an aid in spinning the pace along and spotting unexpected comedy.

With Jack Carson and Dennis Morgan

The Damned Don't Cry

A Warner Brothers Picture

(1950)

CAST: Joan Crawford, David Brian, Steve Cochran, Kent Smith, Hugh Sanders, Selena Royle, Jacqueline de Wit, Morris Ankrum, Edith Evanson, Richard Egan, Jimmy Moss, Sara Perry, Eddie Marr.

CREDITS: Story by Gertrude Walker. Screenplay by Harold Medford and Jerome Weidman. Produced by Jerry Wald. Directed by Vincent Sherman. Cameraman, Ted McCord. Art Director, Robert Haas. Music by Daniele Amfitheatrof. Wardrobe, Sheila O'Brien. Editor, Rudi Fehr. Running time, 103 minutes.

SYNOPSIS

Ethel Whitehead (Joan Crawford) is fed up with poverty, her drab parents, her laborer husband, Roy (Richard Egan), and her dull existence in a factory town. When her only child is killed in a bicycle accident, she decides there is more to life than this and leaves her family, to try her luck in another city. Working at a cigar counter, she meets a meek, colorless but talented accountant, Martin Blackford (Kent Smith), and spurs him on to a more ambitious career. Meanwhile, she herself has become a clothes model for buyers and a date-for-pay gal on the side. Blackford falls in love with Ethel, and she pushes him into the good graces of a night-club owner whose accounting hang-ups Martin unravels as if by magic. This leads Ethel and Blackford on to an encounter with George Castleman (David Brian), who runs a ruthless crime cartel. Ethel, holding out to Blackford the promise of eventual marriage if he goes along with her ambitions for him, persuades him to become Castleman's chief accountant, though his conservative nature quails at the sordid aspects of his employer's occupation. Castleman's wife (Edith Evanson) is an invalid and he has a wandering eye. Impressed by Ethel's spirit and drive, he hires down-at-the-heels socialite Patricia Longworth (Selena Royle) to give Ethel, who by now has become his mistress, some polish, travel, and cultivation. Then he sets her

With Steve Cochran

With Richard Egan

With David Brian and Kent Smith

up as Lorna Hansen Forbes, a "Texas heiress." Lorna and Patricia make the top society columns, travel in the highest international circles. She is now in love with Castleman, who, having perfected his Galatea, disenchants her by attempting a shocking form of utilization. Beneath his cultivated veneer and studied good manners, Castleman is a brutal, unscrupulous power-seeker. He plans to use Lorna (née Ethel) to rub out his arch-rival Nick Prenta (Steve Cochran), who lives in a western city. Lorna, sent west to trap Prenta, falls in love with him. She deliberately delays the evolvement of Castleman's original trap-Prenta strategy. Blackford comes west to warn her not to dally. Castleman, sensing the change in Lorna's attitude, also shows up, and he and Prenta shoot it out. Blackford saves Lorna's life by persuading Castleman that she may yet be useful. Lorna escapes, however, and drives away aimlessly, landing finally in the little town where her life began. Castleman follows and shoots and wounds her as Lorna, now reverted to Ethel, calmly walks out the door of her old home to face him. She has decided that fear is worse

than death. Castleman is killed in a cross fire by Blackford, and at the end Ethel's fate is in doubt. It is presumed that it won't be a happy one.

What the critics said about
THE DAMNED DON'T CRY

Bosley Crowther in the New York Times

Miss Crawford runs through the whole routine of cheap motion-picture dramatics in her latter-day hard-boiled, dead-pan style. As a laborer's wife, she plays it without makeup and with her face heavily greased. As a cigar store clerk and clothes model, she plays it tough. . . . And as the ultimately cultivated "lady," she gives it all the lofty dignity that goes with champagne buckets and Palm Springs swimming pools. A more artificial lot of acting could hardly be achieved.

Howard Barnes in the New York Herald Tribune

The scenario has given Miss Crawford ample scope to emote and show her charms. If it is contrived, it is because the theme is shabby and the incidents too violent for complete plausibility.

Harriet Craig

A Columbia Picture

(1950)

CAST: Joan Crawford, Wendell Corey, Lucille Watson, Allyn Joslyn, William Bishop, K. T. Stevens, Viola Roache, Raymond Greenleaf, Ellen Corby, Fiona O'Shiel, Patric Mitchell, Virginia Brissac, Katherine Warren, Douglas Wood, Kathryn Card, Charles Evans, Mira McKinney.

CREDITS: Based on the play "Craig's Wife" by George Kelly. Screenplay by Anne Froelick and James Gunn. Produced by William Dozier. Directed by Vincent Sherman. Cameraman, Joseph Walker. Art Director, Walter Holscher. Music by Morris T. Stoloff. Wardrobe, Sheila O'Brien. Editor, Viola Lawrence. Running time, 94 minutes.

SYNOPSIS

Harriet Craig (Joan Crawford) is a domineering shrew whose only real love is her meticulously kept and richly appointed house. Her husband Walter (Wendell Corey) must accordingly accept second place in the domestic scheme of things and as he is an easy-going, affectionate type, it takes him some time to realize his wife's monstrous selfishness and essential hatred of men, a syndrome initiated in girlhood when her irresponsible father deserted her mother and herself. A neurotic perfectionist, and a stickler for absolute cleanliness, Harriet makes it impossible for Walter to feel at ease in his own home. She does not really love her husband; Harriet wishes to run his life without regard for his wishes or feelings, and when it appears that he will get a new assignment from his boss that will interfere with her own domestic status quo she ruthlessly undermines with his employer this husband toward whom, on the surface, she professes loving concern and sympathy. When her young cousin, Clare (K. T. Stevens), falls in love with Wes Miller (William Bishop), Harriet, for her own good reasons, sees fit to break it up. Harriet also disapproves of Walter's comfortable old-shoe friendship with easy-going Billy Birkmire (Allyn Joslyn), and succeeds in keeping Billy away from the house. Eventually, Walter begins to get intimations of his wife's true nature, and when he finally sees the light, he smashes her favorite vase and walks out, leaving Harriet to her only true love—her house.

What the critics said about HARRIET CRAIG

In Variety

Joan Crawford does a prime job of putting over the selfish title-character, equipping it with enough sock to cloak the obviousness that motivates the dramatics. Over the years, plot has lost freshness, but script up-dating, the strong playing, and direction add a sheen that keeps it interesting.

Otis L. Guernsey, Jr. in the New York Herald Tribune

With unidentified players and Lucille Watson

The film gives authentic movie star Joan Crawford an opportunity to command the camera's attention through an authentic star role. She remains, as always, a stylish performer in her clear and forceful characterization. . . . Her vehicle may be somewhat laborious but it is steady enough to carry Miss Crawford's act. . . . In every mannerism of speech or gesture, Miss Crawford suggests that she is a queen in the country of the cinema, playing a dominant woman whose unkindly rule of her home has psychotic origins.

Goodbye My Fancy

A Warner Brothers Picture

(1951)

CAST: Joan Crawford, Robert Young, Frank Lovejoy, Eve Arden, Janice Rule, Lurene Tuttle, Howard St. John, Viola Roache, Ellen Corby, Morgan Farley, Virginia Gibson, John Qualen, Ann Robin, Mary Carver.

CREDITS: Based on the play by Fay Kanin. Screenplay by Ivan Goff and Ben Roberts. Produced by Henry Blanke. Directed by Vincent Sherman. Cameraman, Ted McCord. Art Director, Stanley Fleischer. Music by Ray Heindorf. Wardrobe by Sheila O'Brien. Running time, 107 minutes.

SYNOPSIS

Agatha Reed (Joan Crawford), a congresswoman, returns to her alma mater, from which she had been expelled twenty years before, in order to receive an honorary degree. She accepts the invitation with alacrity, since she wishes to

With Robert Young

With Howard St. John and Robert Young

see once more her former love, Dr. James Merrill (Robert Young), now the college president. When she was a student and he a young professor, she had lost her scholastic standing because of an all-night date with him. They have not seen each other in years. Of course the romantic fires are rekindled when Agatha and Jim meet again. Complications are forthcoming from magazine photographer Matt Cole (Frank Lovejoy), who is in love with Agatha and has followed her in her journeys around the world. Matt feels he and Agatha belong together, and that her feeling for Jim is a holdover memory from the past that she has not completely resolved. A subtheme deals with one of the professors, Dr. Pitt (Morgan Farley), who wants to introduce more progressive teaching methods and has to contend with the reactionary conservatism of school trustee Claude Griswold (Howard St. John) and his wife, Ellen (Lurene Tuttle). Agatha gets involved in the struggle when she sides with Dr. Pitt; this creates a number of misunderstandings with others, in the course of which she realizes she is better suited to Matt than to Jim, and finally lays to rest the romantic memory she has carried for years.

What the critics said about
GOODBYE, MY FANCY
In Variety

Performances are very slick, under Vincent Sherman's direction. Miss Crawford, recently involved in only heavily dramatic roles, sustains the romantic, middle-aged congresswoman with a light touch that is excellent.

Bosley Crowther in the New York Times

When Miss Crawford makes a mighty effort to do what she obviously regards as a significant piece of performing, the atmosphere is electrically charged. . . . For the lady is famously given to striking aggressive attitudes and to carrying herself in a manner that is formidable and cold. That is the principal misfortune of *Goodbye My Fancy*. Miss Crawford's errant congresswoman is as aloof and imposing as the capital dome.

With Frank Lovejoy and Robert Young

With three unidentified cast members

With Dennis Morgan

This Woman Is Dangerous
A Warner Brothers Picture
(1952)

CAST: Joan Crawford, Dennis Morgan, David Brian, Richard Webb, Mari Aldon, Philip Carey, Ian MacDonald, Katherine Warren, George Chandler, William Challee, Sherry Jackson, Stuart Randall, Douglas Fowley.

CREDITS: Original story by Bernard Firard. Screenplay by Geoffrey Homes and George Worthing Yates. Produced by Robert Sisk. Directed by Felix Feist. Cameraman, Ted McCord. Art Director, Leo K. Kuter. Music by David Buttolph. Wardrobe by Sheila O'Brien. Editor, James C. Moore. Running time, 97 minutes.

SYNOPSIS

Beth Austin (Joan Crawford) is the mastermind of a holdup gang and the mistress of its most cold-blooded killer, Matt Jackson (David Brian). After pulling the carefully planned and executed holdup of a New Orleans gambling house, Beth, who has been suffering for some time from failing eyesight, goes to a hospital in a distant state for a curative operation. Jackson, a violent man and a possessive lover, agrees to hide out while impatiently awaiting her recovery. The FBI gets a clue to her whereabouts and begins tracing her to the hospital. The doctor who treats her is Ben Halleck (Dennis Morgan), and the forced association with him during her operative and recovery periods breeds a mutual love that far surpasses in her mind the wild feeling she once had for Matt. Matt, however, becomes suspicious of her long hospital stay and puts a private eye on her trail. When Beth, who has inwardly reformed by now, realizes that she is endangering Ben by continuing to encourage him, she renounces him, and then tries to reach Matt in time to prevent her jealous ex-lover from doing any harm to Ben. The climax finds the principal actors all in the hospital, where an enraged Matt, looking for Beth and Ben, has taken a last stand in the observation room over the operating theater. Here he plans to draw a bead on the man who displaced him in Beth's affections. The FBI men move in, just in time, and Matt's plan is thwarted. Beth is promised leniency, and plans for a life with Ben after a short prison sentence.

What the critics said about
THIS WOMAN IS DANGEROUS

Bosley Crowther in the New York Times

When trouble comes to Joan Crawford in her motion picture roles, it comes in great big agonizing hunks. . . . The incredibly durable star, whose theatrical personality has now reached the ossified stage, appears as a woman criminal. . . . There is only one possible explanation for such

With Mari Aldon and Philip Carey

fictitious junk as this, which is willfully delivered in the name of dramatic fare. That is as pure contrivance for the display of Miss Crawford's stony charm. Those who admire the actress may be most tenderly moved by the evidence of the suffering she stolidly undergoes. And to these the arrant posturing of Miss Crawford may seem the quintessence of acting art. But for people of mild discrimination and even moderate reasonableness, the suffering of Miss Crawford will be generously matched by their own in the face of *This Woman Is Dangerous.*

Otis Guernsey, Jr. in the New York Herald Tribune

Joan Crawford runs through a series of problems concerning everything from the operating table to gangsterism in a long, windy, and tiresome story. *This Woman Is Dangerous* is a film of many pretenses but little conviction.

With unidentified child actor and Dennis Morgan

With Dennis Morgan

Sudden Fear

Produced by Joseph Kaufman
for RKO Radio Pictures

(1952)

CAST: Joan Crawford, Jack Palance, Gloria Grahame, Bruce Bennett, Virginia Huston, Touch Connors.

CREDITS: Based on the novel by Edna Sherry. Screenplay by Lenore Coffee and Robert Smith. Produced by Joseph Kaufman. Directed by David Miller. Cameraman, Charles Lang, Jr. Art Director, Boris Leven. Music composed and directed by Elmer Bernstein. Wardrobe by Sheila O'Brien. Editor, Leon Barsha. Running time, 110 minutes.

SYNOPSIS

Myra Hudson (Joan Crawford) is a wealthy playwright who finds it necessary to fire an actor, Lester Blaine (Jack Palance), during a New York rehearsal of one of her plays. Later she meets him by accident on a train headed for her home in San Francisco. Lester makes himself agreeable, they date, and shortly she is in love with him. Soon he has inveigled her into marrying him, and for a while she is sublimely happy. She plans to make a will leaving Lester well provided for, but with the bulk of her fortune left to a foundation. She makes the mistake of telling him this. Shortly before the foundation agreement is to be signed, Myra is working with a jammed tape recorder in her library and overhears, via an accidental playback, a conversation between Lester and Irene Neves (Gloria Grahame), a girl friend who has followed him to San Francisco from New York. They are plotting Myra's murder, though with no decisive plan in mind. A horrified Myra spends a sleepless night, first in terror, then with a gathering desire for retaliation. Her imaginative playwright's mind gets to work, and she conceives a complex and diabolical scheme to outplay Lester and Irene in a series of steps that will lead finally to framing Irene for Lester's murder. Meanwhile, for several days she must act a part and outplay her husband and his mistress, destroying them before they destroy her. At the denouement, as she is planning to murder Lester in Irene's apartment with Irene's gun, she is detected prematurely by Lester and the truth begins to dawn on him. Myra flees down a hilly San Francisco street and as she is wearing a scarf and coat similar to Irene's, who is walking in the opposite direction, Lester, in a panic, confuses Irene with Myra and runs her down with his car, killing them both. Myra witnesses the accident, hears her husband and his mistress pronounced dead, and returns home numbed, but purged and liberated.

With Jack Palance

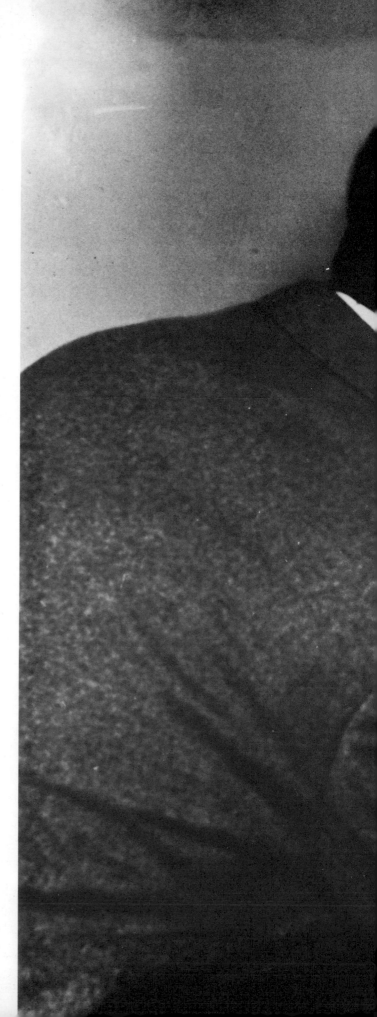

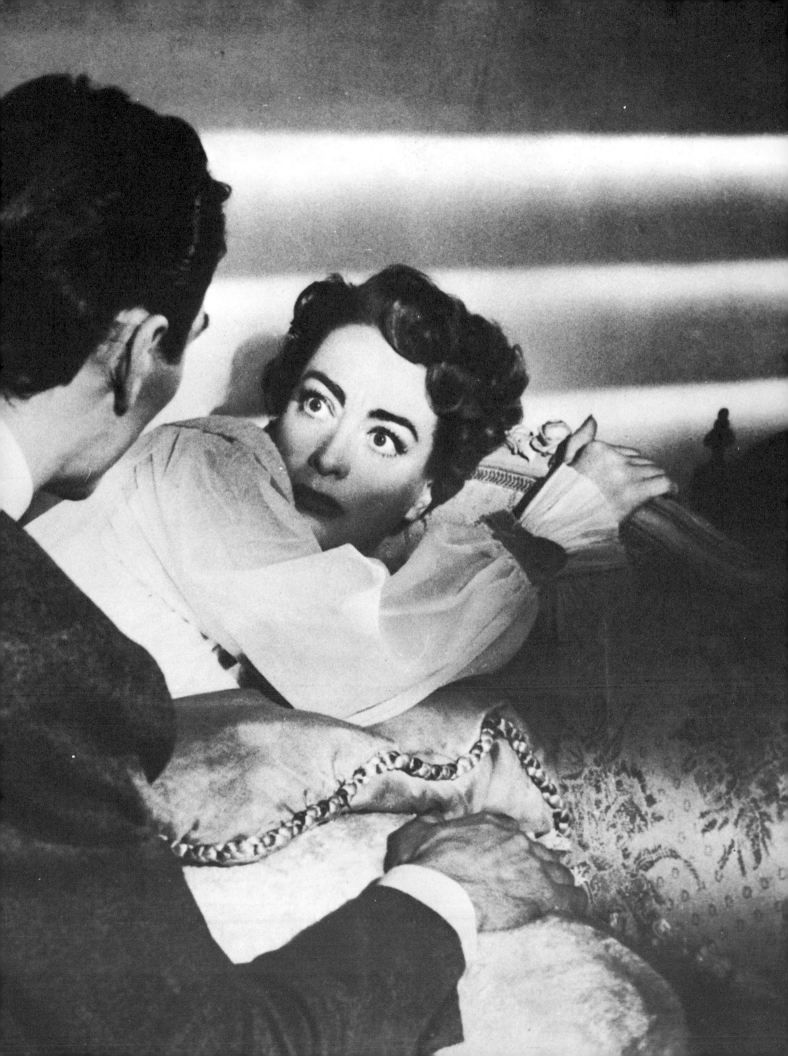

What the critics said about SUDDEN FEAR

A. H. Weiler in the New York Times

Joan Crawford should be credited with a truly professional performance. [She] does notably well in an exercise which involves practically all the emotions. . . . She behaves in a convincing manner.

Otis L. Guernsey, Jr. in the New York Herald Tribune

The scenario . . . is designed to allow Miss Crawford a wide range of quivering reactions to vicious events, as she passes through the stage of starry-eyed love, terrible disillusionment, fear, hatred, and finally hysteria. With her wide eyes and forceful bearing, she is the woman for the job.

With Touch Connors, Jack Palance, Bruce Bennett, and Gloria Grahame

With Jack Palance

With Jack Palance

With Michael Wilding

Torch Song

A Metro-Goldwyn-Mayer Picture

(1953)

CAST: Joan Crawford, Michael Wilding, Gig Young, Marjorie Rambeau, Henry Morgan, Dorothy Patrick, James Todd, Eugene Loring, Paul Guilfoyle, Benny Rubin, Peter Chong, Maidie Norman, Nancy Gates, Chris Warfield, Rudy Render.

CREDITS: From the story "Why Should I Cry?" by I. A. R. Wylie. Screenplay by John Michael Hayes and Jan Lustig. Produced by Henry Berman and Sidney Franklin, Jr. Directed by Charles Walters. Cameraman, Robert Planck. Art Director, Cedric Gibbons. Music by Adolph Deutsch. Costumes by Helen Rose. Editor, Albert Akst. Running time, 90 minutes.

SYNOPSIS

Jenny Stewart (Joan Crawford) is a hard-as-nails and utterly selfish musical comedy star, a neurotic perfectionist in her work who wants to dominate everyone and everything around her. As such, she is a great trial to her co-workers. A blind pianist, Tye Graham (Michael Wilding), is drafted for temporary rehearsal duty when her exasperated pianist quits. Soon the imperious Jenny and Tye are at odds as he courteously but relentlessly criticizes her arbitrary song stylings and ruthless ways. Deep down in the defensively egotistical Jenny is a lonely, yearning person who wants a deep and meaningful love relationship, but is disenchanted with the men she knows, including Broadway parasite Cliff Willard (Gig Young). At first she fights her growing love for Tye, who continues to irritate her with his probing, accurate criticisms. While on a visit to her mother's (Marjorie Rambeau) she goes through a scrapbook and finds Tye's byline on an old review. It seems that he had fallen in love with her when he was a second-string dramatic critic and had seen her in one of her first shows; in his review he refers to her as a "gypsy madonna." Martha (Dorothy Patrick), in love with Tye, arouses Jenny's jealousy. Tye, however, having never seen Martha, cannot return her love. But before being blinded in World War II he had seen Jenny and carried the memory of her in his heart for years. Jenny, realizing now that she is loved and loving at last in the complete and final way she has always craved, goes to Tye and confesses her need of him. His own resistance is broken, now that she has revealed her tender, yielding side, and they embrace.

NOTE: This was Joan Crawford's first Metro-Goldwyn-Mayer picture in ten years. It was photographed in handsome color, and she sang and danced several solos and production numbers. Her voice was dubbed in by India Adams.

What one critic said about TORCH SONG

Otis L. Guernsey, Jr. in the New York Herald Tribune

Joan Crawford has another of her star-sized roles. . . . Playing a musical comedy actress in the throes of rehearsal and in love with a blind pianist, she is vivid and irritable, volcanic and feminine. She dances; she pretends to sing; she graciously permits her wide mouth and snappish eyes to be photographed in Technicolor. . . . Here is Joan Crawford all over the screen, in command, in love and in color, a real movie star in what amounts to a carefully produced one-woman show. Miss Crawford's acting is sheer and colorful as a painted arrow, aimed straight at the sensibilities of her particular fans.

With Gig Young

With Michael Wilding

With cast members

Johnny Guitar

A Republic Picture

(1954)

CAST: Joan Crawford, Sterling Hayden, Mercedes McCambridge, Scott Brady, Ward Bond, Ben Cooper, Ernest Borgnine, John Carradine, Royal Dano, Frank Ferguson, Paul Fix, Rhys Williams, Ian MacDonald.

CREDITS: Based on the novel by Roy Chanslor. Screenplay by Philip Yordan. Produced by Herbert J. Yates. Directed by Nicholas Ray. Cameraman, Harry Stradling. Art Director, James Sullivan. Music by Victor Young. Song by Peggy Lee and Victor Young. Wardrobe by Sheila O'Brien. Editor, Richard L. Van Enger. Running time, 110 minutes.

SYNOPSIS

Vienna (Joan Crawford), a beautiful and aggressive lady of fortune, builds a gambling saloon in the wilds of Arizona, which she manages successfully. With shrewd foresight, she has chosen a site where a railroad will soon be coming through. Accordingly, her prosperity-oriented plans bring upon her the hatred of a neighboring town, led by boss John McIvers (Ward Bond). McIvers' ally is Emma Small (Mercedes McCambridge), a bitter, sexually frustrated woman who, along with McIvers, is determined to keep the area an open range for cattle. Vienna is carrying on an affair with the "Dancin' Kid" (Scott Brady), the leader of a gang of miners who have converted themselves into bank robbers. Into this environment comes a loner, Johnny Guitar (Sterling Hayden). Johnny goes gunless because he tends to be

With Frank Ferguson

With Scott Brady, Royal Dano

trigger-happy and doesn't want to kill anyone. Vienna and Johnny meet and gradually fall in love. Soon Johnny finds himself compelled to strap on his gun again to protect Vienna from the ever more angry cattle people. Spurred on by John and Emma, they seek to drive Vienna out of the territory and destroy her saloon. Posses pursue Vienna, threats are made, and other harassments are visited on her. Emma continues to fan the townspeople's anger into fierce flames by insisting that incoming settlers and fences will ruin their economy. Vienna confronts her enemies, and she and Emma square off for a duel to the death, from which Vienna emerges unharmed. Johnny organizes resistance to the posses and overcomes

them, and he and Vienna plan for the future.

What one critic said about JOHNNY GUITAR
Brog in Variety

It proves [Miss Crawford] should leave saddles and Levis to someone else and stick to city lights for a background. [The film] is only a fair piece of entertainment. [The scriptwriter] becomes so involved with character nuances and neuroses, all wrapped up in dialogue, that [the picture] never has a chance to rear up in the saddle. . . . The people in the story never achieve much depth, this character shallowness being at odds with the pretentious attempt at analysis to which the script and direction devotes so much time.

Female on the Beach

A Universal-International Picture

(1955)

CAST: Joan Crawford, Jeff Chandler, Jan Sterling, Cecil Kellaway, Natalie Schafer, Charles Drake, Judith Evelyn, Stuart Randall, Marjorie Bennett, Romo Vincent.

CREDITS: Based on the play "The Besieged Heart" by Robert Hill. Screenplay by Robert Hill and Richard Alan Simmons. Produced by Albert Zugsmith. Directed by Joseph Pevney. Cameraman, Charles Lang. Art Director, Alexander Golitzen. Music by Joseph Gershenson. Wardrobe by Sheila O'Brien. Editor, Russell Schoengarth. Running time, 97 minutes.

SYNOPSIS

Lynn Markham (Joan Crawford) is a rich and lonely widow, whose late husband, a Las Vegas gambler, has left her a beach house she has never visited. She comes to Balboa Beach to take over the house and meets Amy Rawlinson (Jan Sterling), a real estate woman whose behavior seems mysterious. Even more mysterious is Drummond ("Drummy") Hall (Jeff Chandler), a handsome beach-bum who wanders in and out of the house as though he owned it. Lynn learns that the house had previously been rented by Amy to an older woman, Eloise Crandall (Judith Evelyn), who died mysteriously in a fall from the balcony overlooking the beach. According to Lieutenant Galley (Charles Drake), a detective who appears in the house at unexpected times, there is no certainty whether the Crandall death was murder, suicide, or accident. Lynn is attracted to Drummy, even though she has spotted him as a type who wants an easy life. Drummy, it develops, is teamed with card sharps Osbert and Queenie Sorenson (Cecil Kellaway and Natalie Schafer). Though Lynn knows that Drummy probably spells trouble, she finally gives in to him, after at first resisting, and shortly she is in love. Then, by accident, she comes upon Eloise Crandall's hidden diary; in it she reads the sordid details of Drummy's calculating pursuit of Eloise to set her up for card games with Queenie and Osbert. Through Eloise's eyes she sees Drummy for what he is, a weakling and the dupe of his shrewder allies. Disenchanted, she tries again to break with him but finds the physical attraction too strong. Meanwhile, it develops that Amy Rawlinson is also in love with Drummy and has been chasing him, though he continually rebuffs her. Lynn ignores the warnings of the detective, Galley, and she and Drummy are married. A series of coincidental events on her honeymoon night leaves Lynn with the impression that Drummy murdered Eloise and has the same fate in mind for her. It develops, however, that the real killer was Amy, who wanted Drummy for herself.

With Jeff Chandler

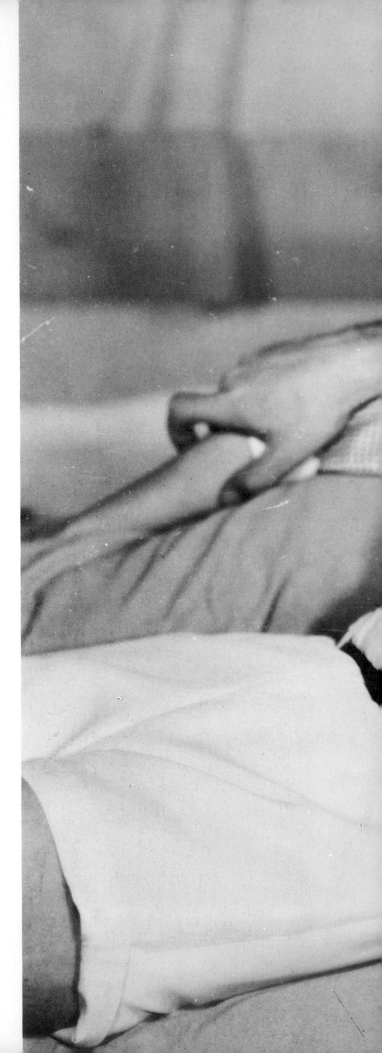

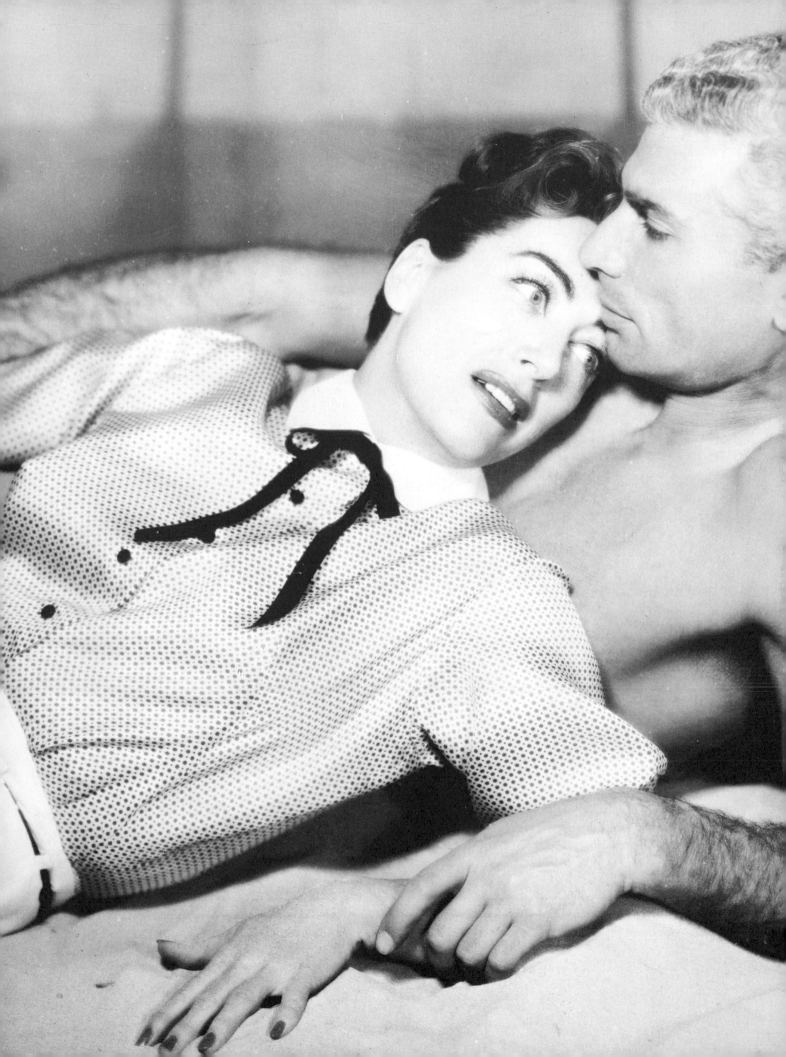

With Jeff Chandler, Natalie Schafer, and Cecil Kellaway

With Jeff Chandler

What the critics said about
FEMALE ON THE BEACH

Brog in Variety

Meat of the dramatics falls to Miss Crawford and Chandler and they deliver well. . . . Joseph Pevney's direction gets quite a bit out of the players in putting them through the paces set by [the script].

Bosley Crowther in the New York Times

Miss Crawford and Mr. Chandler labor grimly toward a storm-lashed climactic scene. Their progress is rendered no more fetching by the inanities of a hackneyed script and the artificiality and pretentiousness of Miss Crawford's acting style.

With Jeff Chandler

Queen Bee

A Columbia Picture

(1955)

CAST: Joan Crawford, Barry Sullivan, Betsy Palmer, John Ireland, Lucy Marlow, William Leslie, Fay Wray, Katherine Anderson, Tim Hovey, Linda Bennett, Willa Pearl Curtis, Bill Walker, Olan Soule.

CREDITS: Based on the novel by Edna Lee. Screenplay by Ranald MacDougall. Directed by Mr. MacDougall. Produced by Jerry Wald. Cameraman, Charles Lang. Art Director, Ross Bellah. Music, Morris Stoloff. Gowns, Jean Louis. Editor, Viola Lawrence. Running time, 95 minutes.

SYNOPSIS

Eva Phillips (Joan Crawford) is an outwardly personable but inwardly evil and depraved woman. She has a compulsion to dominate everyone around her in order to promote her own selfish aims. She is likened by one of her victims to the queen bee of a hive, who stings to death any rivals that might challenge her position. Eva presides imperiously over the Georgia mansion of her husband, Avery Phillips (Barry Sullivan), a wealthy mill owner who has taken refuge in drink out of hatred for his wife. A cousin, Jennifer Stewart (Lucy Marlow), comes to visit the Phillipses and at first is beguiled by Eva's charm and affability. Gradually Jennifer comes to learn the monstrous truth about Eva, and watches in horrified fascination as Eva maneuvers to prevent the marriage of Avery's sister, Carol Lee Phillips (Betsy Pal-

With Barry Sullivan and John Ireland

mer)., to Judson Prentiss (John Ireland), who manages the estate. Judson, it develops, has been the lover of the "queen bee," who still regards him as her private property and tries to lure him into renewed love-making. When Carol learns the truth about Judson and Eva, she commits suicide. Eva continues to taunt and ridicule her husband, whose disenchantment with her galls her proud spirit. Gradually, Jennifer and Avery are drawn together, and love grows between them. Eva senses the developing romance and increases her assorted malevolences. Finally, Judson, thoroughly repelled by Eva's behavior, guilt-ridden because of his own betrayal of Carol, and determined to avenge her suicide even if it involves the sacrifice of his own life, takes Eva out driving and deliberately crashes, killing them both. Thus, he leaves Avery and Jennifer free to love each other.

What the critics said about QUEEN BEE

Bosley Crowther in the New York Times

As the wife of a Southern mill owner whom she has driven to bitterness and drink by her ruthless, self-seeking machinations and frank infidelity [Miss Crawford] is the height of mellifluous meanness and frank insincerity. When she is killed at the end, as she should be, it is a genuine pleasure and relief.

William K. Zinsser in the New York Herald Tribune

[The film] takes its title from the lady of the hive, Joan Crawford, who stings her rivals to death so that she can have the drones all to herself. . . . Miss Crawford plays her role with such silky villainy that we long to see her dispatched.

With John Ireland

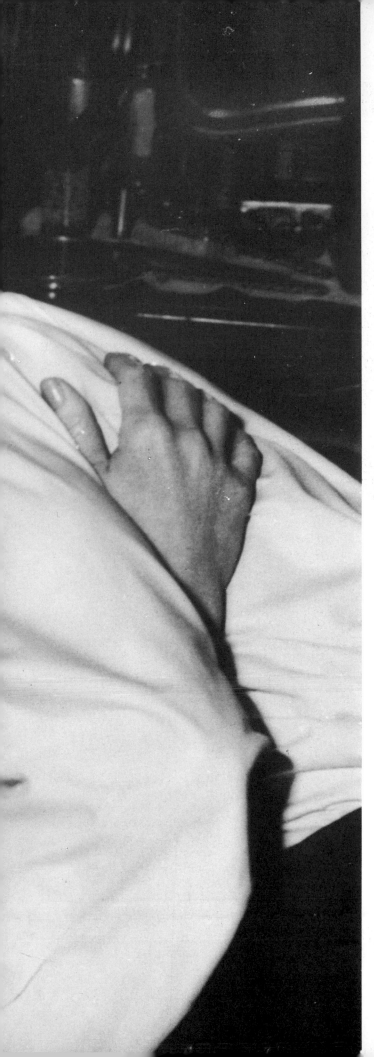

Autumn Leaves

A William Goetz Production
for Columbia Pictures

(1956)

CAST: Joan Crawford, Cliff Robertson, Vera Miles, Lorne Greene, Ruth Donnelly, Sheppard Strudwick, Selmer Jackson, Maxine Cooper, Marjorie Bennett, Frank Gerstle, Leonard Mudie, Maurice Manson, Bob Hopkins.

CREDITS: Story and screenplay by Jack Jevne, Lewis Meltzer, and Robert Blees. Produced by William Goetz. Directed by Robert Aldrich. Cameraman, Charles Lang. Art Director, Bill Glasgow. Music composed by Hans Salter. Conductor, Morris Stoloff. Gowns, Jean Louis. Editor, Michael Luciano. Running time, 108 minutes.

SYNOPSIS

Millicent Wetherby (Joan Crawford) is an attractive but frustrated New Englander in her early forties, who transplants to California after the death of her invalid father (Selmer Jackson). Because she had had to nurse her father over so many years, her marital chances have diminished. Lonely and heart-hungry, but disciplined and valiant, Milly is self-employed as a manuscript typist. She lives in a drab bungalow court where her only friend is the brusque but kindhearted superintendent, Liz Eckhardt (Ruth Donnelly). Though some men find Milly attractive, she gets no advances because they feel she must be dated up. One of her customers gives her a ticket to a concert, where she sits alone through a Chopin piano recital, reliving with tear-filled eyes her lonely dreams and her deep emotional needs. Later, determined not to go back to the bungalow court, she goes to a crowded restaurant where she finds herself sitting opposite an equally lonely young man in his late twenties, Burt Hanson (Cliff Robertson). Burt escorts her home; later, he takes her to the beach, tells her he loves her, and suggests marriage. But Milly, sensitive, fearful, distrustful of love, and conscious of the difference in their ages, sends him away. Lonely weeks follow for them both; then one day Burt reappears. Unable to resist his persistent wooing, Milly marries him. A series of shocking revelations ensues, as Burt is caught in outrageous lies. Though he has denied any previous marriage, his ex-wife Virginia (Vera Miles) appears. She reveals that she had divorced Burt, without his knowledge, only weeks before his marriage to Milly; hence, he has barely escaped bigamy. Virginia has come to seek a property settlement, and steers the increasingly puzzled and alarmed Milly to Burt's father (Lorne Greene), whom Milly finds enigmatic and strange. Burt begins exhibiting signs of melancholia and kleptomania, and becomes upset when Milly sug-

With Cliff Robertson

gests that he go to see his father. When he does go, after much pressuring from Milly, he finds his father and Virginia living together. It develops that the original revelation of Burt's father's liaison with Virginia caused the estrangement between her and Burt, and sowed the seeds of Burt's mental aberration. Burt goes into severe depression cycles, followed by attacks of paranoid suspicion of Milly and almost homicidal violence directed at her. Milly is forced to consult a psychiatrist, who recommends a sanitarium for Burt. Eventually she is compelled to have him committed, working overtime to pay his hospital bills. When she finally learns that he is cured, she dreads seeing him again, feeling that now that he no longer needs her, he will reject her. But Burt brings her a fresh happiness by telling her he now loves her more than ever.

What the critics said about AUTUMN LEAVES

Lawrence J. Quirk in Motion Picture Herald

The heart-appeal is accentuated throughout, and with a moving eloquence kept within fine margins of restraint, thanks to director Robert Aldrich's control over a taut, well-knit, extremely literate script. . . . Miss Crawford as an aging "career girl" who brushes aside all doubts and guilt feelings to marry a man much younger, Cliff Robertson, brings to her latest role all the acting resources she has cultivated so successfully in 31 years of picture-making. As the lonely and heart-hungry but proud and valiant woman entering the autumnal years, she is moving and eloquent in her slow and hesitant acceptance of the love proffered by Robertson. As the wife who makes the horrifying discovery that she has married a very complex, tortured and confused young man sliding rapidly into the dark world of schizophrenia, she is brilliantly bewildered in her disenchantment, forceful and decisive when she decides to commit him to an institution, and eloquently tormented in heart and mind when she realizes that his eventual cure may rob her of his love and need for her which sent him reeling in her direction in the first place.

William K. Zinsser in the New York Herald Tribune

The film is a mature study of loneliness and mental distress. On the whole Robert Aldrich has directed the film with good intentions. He has tried to explore the minds of his characters. . . . Miss Crawford is as attractive as ever, and she brings the whole spectrum of emotions to her role. In her early scenes she is so afraid of being hurt that she is visibly tense and almost hostile. This is a good portrait of the career girl who has been single too long. . . . The strength of Miss Crawford's performance is that it is natural and controlled. A lesser actress would bring more than a tinge of ham to such a juicy role.

The Story of Esther Costello

A Romulus Production for Valiant Films
Released by Columbia Pictures

(1957)

CAST: Joan Crawford, Rossano Brazzi, Heather Sears, Lee Patterson, Ron Randell, Fay Compton, John Loder, Denis O'Dea, Sidney James, Bessie Love, Robert Ayres, Maureen Delaney, Harry Hutchinson, Tony Quinn, Janina Faye, Estelle Brody, June Clyde, Sally Smith, Diana Day, Megs Jenkins, Andrew Cruikshank, Victor Rietti, Sheila Manahan.

CREDITS: A Romulus Production. From the novel by Nicholas Monsarrat. Screenplay by Charles Kaufman. Produced and directed by David Miller. Cameraman, Robert Krasker. Art Directors, George Provis, Tony Masters. Music by Lambert Williamson. Gowns by Jean Louis. Editor, Ralph Kemplen. Running time, 127 minutes.

SYNOPSIS

Margaret Landi (Joan Crawford), a wealthy American woman separated from her philandering husband, Carlo (Rossano Brazzi), visits her childhood home in Ireland where she encounters a young girl, Esther Costello (Heather Sears), who has been rendered deaf, blind, and speechless by a childhood accident. The affliction, induced by shock, is psychosomatic rather than physical. The girl lives under squalid conditions and is improperly cared for. The village priest (Denis O'Dea) uses psychology to inveigle the at first reluctant Margaret into taking an interest in the girl. Childless, her marriage in ashes, Margaret is lured into this unexpected emotional outlet and becomes the girl's patron. They travel together, looking for methods of helping Esther. Margaret learns Braille and a sign language with her, and after some discouraging initial attempts at communication, the girl begins to blossom. Soon Esther is a celebrated case of triumph over unusual adversity and she and Margaret are in demand for functions and drives. Reenter Carlo, who inveigles the still smitten Margaret into returning to him. Then he seeks to use the girl's growing reputation for cheap financial gain in a series of exploitative tours arranged with the help of a mercenary manager, Wenzel (Ron Randell). A young reporter, Harry Grant (Lee Patterson), who has been assigned to cover Esther during her tours, falls in love with her, and she with him. Carlo, a chronic womanizer, lusts after the attractively helpless Esther, and in Margaret's temporary absence from their apartment, rapes her, shocking the girl into a return of her physical faculties. Margaret learns of her husband's business duplicities, and then of the rape. Knowing that Esther's sight, hearing, and speech are now normal, Margaret leaves her with Harry, meets Carlo at the airport after one of his business trips, and drives him and herself to their deaths. Esther and Harry face the future together.

What the critics said about
THE STORY OF ESTHER COSTELLO
William K. Zinsser in the New York Herald Tribune

It wouldn't be a Joan Crawford picture without plenty of anguish—so goes a rigid law of the film industry. And her fans will have their usual good time . . . smiling through their tears, biting their nails, and otherwise purging the emotions. . . . As you can imagine, this plot enables Miss Crawford to run a full-course dinner of dramatic moods, from loneliness to mother love, from pride in the girl to passion with her husband, and finally to smouldering rage when she takes a derringer out of her desk and goes to meet him for the last time. Somehow she pulls it off. This may not be your kind of movie but it is many women's kind of movie and our Joan is queen of the art form.

H. H. T. in the New York Times
It must be said here that Miss Crawford, whose role repeatedly shifts from stage center, is tackling her most becoming assignment in several seasons. Miss Crawford, Mr. Brazzi, Mr. Patterson and all the minor players are professional throughout.

With Rossano Brazzi

With Hope Lange

The Best of Everything

A 20th Century-Fox Picture

(1959)

CAST: Hope Lange, Stephen Boyd, Suzy Parker, Martha Hyer, Diane Baker, Brian Aherne, Robert Evans, Brett Halsey, Donald Harron, Sue Carson, Linda Hutchings, Lionel Kane, Ted Otis, June Blair, Myrna Hansen, Alena Murray, Rachel Stephens, Julie Payne. Louis Jourdan as David Savage. Joan Crawford as Amanda Farrow.

CREDITS: From the novel by Rona Jaffe. Screenplay, Edith Sommer and Mann Rubin. Produced by Jerry Wald. Directed by Jean Negulesco. Cameraman, William C. Mellor. Art Directors, Lyle R. Wheeler, Jack Martin Smith, Mark-Lee Kirk. Music by Alfred Newman. Costumes by Adele Palmer. Editor, Robert Simpson. Running time, 121 minutes.

SYNOPSIS

Amanda Farrow (Joan Crawford) is a waspish, difficult editor in a magazine publishing house. Jaded, negative-minded, embittered and hard, she is involved in a disappointing and unrewarding affair with a married man and tends to take out her assorted discontents on the girls under her charge, including Gregg (Suzy Parker), an aspiring actress who is involved in a destructive, one-sided relationship with a Broadway stage director, David Savage (Louis Jourdan), and an ambitious young secretary, Caroline Bender (Hope Lange), who has just been jilted by her boyfriend and has turned to one of the editors, Mike (Stephen Boyd), for consolation. Amanda bullies Caroline, and runs her down to her superior, Mr. Shalimar (Brian Aherne), but when Amanda decides to forget her married lover (never shown on the screen) and throws up her job to marry a stable widower with several children (this man was never shown on the screen either) Caroline gets her job. Later, Amanda finds she cannot stick the marriage because she has hopelessly lost contact with, or desire for, the simple life; she returns to her old job. Caroline continues at the firm in another editorial post, and decides that she loves Mike, with whom she had temporarily quarreled.

NOTE: There was much criticism over the peripheral role handed Miss Crawford. The men with whom she was supposed to be involved were never shown on the screen. Several of her best scenes, including what was reportedly a superbly acted drunk episode, wound up on the cutting room floor, due to the producer's decision that the film was too long. The synopsis relates principally to Miss Crawford's scenes in the lengthy and multi-charactered film.

What the critics said about
THE BEST OF EVERYTHING

In Variety

Miss Crawford uses her own great authority to give vividness and meaning to a role that is sketchy at best.

Paul V. Beckley in the New York Herald Tribune

You need only watch what happens when the camera turns on Joan Crawford in her role of a mean, nervous, frustrated career woman to see what the picture lacks in general. I know this kind of thing, the woman fighting an uphill battle for love, has been a Crawford specialty in recent years, but experience alone won't explain the electricity. Let's admit first off that the script gives her no more than a fingerhold on the story, that it asks her to navigate in two emotional directions at once, and to make a sudden unaccountable change of character in the denouement, but just the same, when she comes on, you wake up and begin to wonder what's going to happen. You feel badly cheated when it turns out finally that they're not going to let you even take a look at her particular married man and that "rabbit-faced" wife of his. All her problems are worked out off-stage, but even so, restricted to a few mean looks and some vitriolic dialogue, Miss Crawford comes near making the rest of the picture look like a distraction.

With Brian Aherne

What Ever Happened to Baby Jane?

A Seven Arts and Aldrich Production
Released by Warner Brothers

(1962)

CAST: Bette Davis, Joan Crawford, Victor Buono, Marjorie Bennett, Maidie Norman, Anna Lee, Julie Allred, Barbara Merrill, Dave Willock, Gina Gillespie, Ann Barton.

CREDITS: Based on the novel by Henry Farrell. Screenplay by Lukas Heller. Executive Producer, Kenneth Hyman. Associate Producer, Robert Aldrich. Directed by Mr. Aldrich. Cameraman, Ernest Haller. Musical score by Frank DeVol. Costumes by Norma Koch. Art Director, William Glasgow. Edited by Michael Luciano. Running time, 132 minutes.

SYNOPSIS

Jane Hudson (Bette Davis), a former child-star, and her sister Blanche (Joan Crawford), once a top film star, now a cripple retired by a long ago automobile accident, live in isolated circumstances in a crumbling Hollywood home. The cleaning woman, Elvira Stitt (Maidie Norman), has taken note of Jane's increasing instability and heavy drinking and is concerned for Blanche's safety. Jane learns that Blanche is planning to sell the house and place her in a sanitarium. Enraged, she persecutes Blanche in an *outré* manner, serving roasted rodents and boiled parakeets in covered dishes, and preventing her sister from communicating with the outside world. Jane, whose mind is becoming more and more unbalanced, decides to make a comeback by reviving her child-star vaudeville act. She hires Edwin Flagg (Victor Buono), a mother-dominated, porcine character, to help her arrange the music. Edwin goes along with Jane's ridiculous comeback ambitions because he wants the large advance she has promised him. Blanche, who has been locked in her room by Jane, attempts to escape. Jane waylays and mistreats her. Elvira returns, to find Blanche bound to her bed and gagged. Jane kills Elvira in a fit of hysteria. Edwin, while being entertained by Jane, hears the noises made by Blanche upstairs, as she upsets furniture to attract attention. Investigating, he finds Blanche near death and flees the house. Fearful that Edwin has gone to get police aid, Jane takes Blanche to Malibu Beach, where she intends to bury her in the sand. Elvira is reported missing by her family. The police find her body, and a search is instituted for

With Bette Davis

With Bette Davis

With Bette Davis

the missing sisters. Meanwhile, on the beach, Blanche has confessed to Jane that she herself is to blame for the life they have led for years, because, possessed by jealousy of her sister's fame, she had planned the automobile accident which resulted in her being permanently crippled, and had deliberately misled Jane into thinking she was responsible. The police find the sisters on the beach. Jane, her mind finally crumbling, does her Baby Jane act of long ago for the amazed officers and the crowd that has gathered.

What the critics said about
WHAT EVER HAPPENED TO BABY JANE?
Paul V. Beckley in the New York Herald Tribune

If Miss Davis' portrait of an outrageous slattern with the mind of an infant has something of the force of a hurricane, Miss Crawford's performance could be described as the eye of that hurricane, abnormally quiet, perhaps, but ominous and desperate.

Arthur B. Clark in Films in Review

. . . a second viewing of Joan Crawford's performance reveals what hitherto I have not believed, to wit, that she *is* an actress and not merely a beautifully bone-structured personality.

In Variety

Miss Crawford gives a quiet, remarkably fine interpretation of the crippled Blanche, held in emotionally by the nature and temperament of her role. Physically confined to a wheelchair and bed throughout the picture, she has to act from the inside and has her best scenes (because she wisely underplays with Davis) with a maid and those she plays alone. In one superb bit, Miss Crawford reacting to herself on television makes her face fairly glow with the remembrance of fame past. . . . A genuine heartbreaker.

In Motion Picture Herald

In playing their rather implausible roles the two old-pro actresses have a field day under the direction of Robert Aldrich. . . . [Miss Davis] acts throughout . . . with all her well-remembered bite and venom intact, while Miss Crawford plays it beautifully and nobly, as of yore.

In Saturday Review

A superb showcase for the time-ripened talents of two of Hollywood's most accomplished actresses, Bette Davis and Joan Crawford. Scenes that in lesser hands would verge on the ludicrous simply crackle with tension.

With Robert Stack and Herbert Marshall

The Caretakers

United Artists Release of a
Hall Bartlett Production

(1963)

CAST: Robert Stack, Polly Bergen, Joan Crawford, Janis Paige, Diane McBain, Van Williams, Constance Ford, Sharon Hugueny, Herbert Marshall, Robert Vaughn, Ana St. Clair, Barbara Barrie, Susan Oliver, Ellen Corby.

CREDITS: Screenplay by Henry F. Greenberg, from the screen story by Hall Bartlett and Jerry Paris, based on a book by Daniel Telfer. Produced and directed by Hall Bartlett. Music, Elmer Bernstein. Cameraman, Lucien Ballard. Editor, William B. Murphy. Running time, 97 minutes.

SYNOPSIS

Dr. Donovan MacLeod (Robert Stack), a crusading doctor, wishes to prove his theory that many borderline mental cases can be cured through group therapy in positive surroundings. He hopes eventually to establish "day clinics" where patients can be treated by day, returning home at night. Lucretia Terry (Joan Crawford), head nurse at the mental hospital whose superintendent is her long-standing friend Dr. Jubal Harrington (Herbert Marshall), bitterly opposes Dr. Mac-Leod's advanced ideas for group therapy. A rock-bound conservative who believes traditional strait-jacket and padded-cell methods are still the best, Lucretia fights Dr. MacLeod at every turn, is sarcastic at their every confrontation and presides over her nurses' judo sessions. Dr. Harrington, an old-fashioned, weary, and indecisive executive, wavers between the methods the two opponents propose. Nurse Bracker (Constance Ford) is Lucretia's loyal assistant; she shares her superior's views on how the hospital should be run. Nonetheless, Dr. MacLeod's methods gain headway, and his group therapy classes show results. Among his patients are Lorna Melford (Polly Bergen), a disturbed young wife who has gone overboard mentally because her child was killed in a car she was driving; Marion (Janis Paige), a disoriented and neurotic lady of the streets; and such assorted types as a European refugee, a Beatnik, and a senile school teacher. After much trial and error and such harrowing experiences as Lorna's near-rape at the hands of male mental patients into whose ward she had inadvertently wandered, love, understanding, and modern psychiatric methods prevail over the outworn techniques advocated by Lucretia and Dr. Harrington.

What the critics said about THE CARETAKERS

In Time

Fans of medical drama are well aware that when young doctor and old doctor disagree, the young doctor is right. So it takes little ingenuity to know whom to root for when Robert Stack, an earnest young doctor, comes into conflict with Joan Crawford, an aging, hardened head nurse, over how to handle the patients in a mental hospital. . . . After a while, Nurse Crawford's distaste for the proceedings begins to seem understandable.

In Variety

Miss Crawford doesn't so much play her handful of scenes as she dresses for them, looking as if she were en route to a Pepsi board meeting.

Bosley Crowther in the New York Times

Altogether, this woman's melodrama is shallow, showy and cheap—a badly commercial exploitation of very sensitive material. . . . The only thing missing is a slinky exit by Miss Crawford, twirling her chiffons and muttering, "Curses!" . . . Mr. Marshall and Miss Crawford struggle manfully against horrendous odds, which even call for their being named Jubal and Lucretia.

Strait Jacket

A Columbia Pictures Release
of a William Castle Production

(1964)

CAST: Joan Crawford, Diane Baker, Leif Erickson, Howard St. John, John Anthony Hayes, Rochelle Hudson, George Kennedy, Edith Atwater, Mitchell Cox, Lee Yeary, Patricia Krest, Vachel Cos, Patty Lee, Laura Hess, Robert Ward, Lyn Lundgren.

CREDITS: Screenplay by Robert Bloch. Produced and directed by William Castle. Cameraman, Arthur Arling. Editor, Edwin Bryant. Music, Van Alexander. Running time, 93 minutes.

SYNOPSIS

Lucy Harbin (Joan Crawford) is released from a hospital for the criminally insane after twenty years and is reunited with her now-grown daughter, Carol (Diane Baker), who lives with Bill Cutler (Leif Erickson) and his wife, Emily (Rochelle Hudson). Two decades before, Lucy had discovered her young husband and his lady-love of the moment in bed together, and in a rage had hacked them to death with an axe. The crime had been witnessed by Carol, then only three years old. A note of uneasiness and foreboding is struck as soon as Lucy comes home from the hospital. For one thing, Carol wants Lucy to stop dressing in a drab, middle-aged fashion and begin wearing glamorous black wigs and tight-fitting frocks and making like the woman she once was. Lucy feels Carol is trying to brighten her morale by suggesting more youthful apparel, and assumes the manners, appearance, and dress of a woman twenty years younger, with sometimes disconcerting results. A series of incidents reveal that Lucy is still far from well. For one thing, she makes brazen romantic passes at her daughter's handsome young fiancé, Michael Fields (John Anthony Hayes), and when she is taken to visit Michael's snobbish and cautious parents, Mrs. Fields (Edith Atwater) angers Lucy, who goes into a tantrum.

A series of axe murders begins, including that of Leo Krause, the hired man (George Kennedy). Meanwhile, a doctor from the hospital (Mitchell Cox) has looked in on Lucy from time to time and is not satisfied with her progress. Everything seems to point to Lucy as the axe murderess, but at the end it is Carol who is revealed as the killer. Her three-year-old mind, long years before, had registered the murder of her father and his mistress by her mother with a clarity and vividness that in time became pathological, and a saddened Lucy is forced to realize that that long-ago event has made her pathetic daughter a hopeless psychotic.

What the critics said about
STRAIT JACKET

In Time
It must also be the first horror film able to boast that one of its diehard victims (Mitchell Cox) is a real life Vice President of the Pepsi-Cola Company. As for Pepsi-Cola Board Member Crawford, she plainly plays her mad scenes For Those Who Think Jung.

In Variety
Miss Crawford does well by her role, delivering an animated performance.

Judith Crist in the New York Herald Tribune
Strait Jacket should be subtitled *What Ever Happened to Baby Monster?* and there's a clue for you. [It] proves that lightning does not strike twice and that it's time to get Joan Crawford out of those housedress horror B movies and back into haute couture. Miss Crawford, you see, is high class. Too high class to withstand in mufti the banality of Robert Bloch's script, cheap-jack production, inept and/or vacuous supporting players and direction better suited to the mist-and-cobweb idiocies of the Karloff school of suspense. These make a disappointing, low-level melodrama of this madness-and-murder tale that might have been a thriller, given Class A treatment. . . . Miss Crawford is without peer when it comes to diffident neuroses, valiant tears, and prideful motherhood, and she's awfully good to look at even in her gray-haired, dishevelled, fresh-from-the-asylum drabness. But what she does need here is a peer or two to sustain the credibility of the build-up as well as the final twist.

In the Daily News
The star is hampered by a script riddled with clichés.

Elaine Rothschild in Films in Review
I must say I am full of admiration for Joan Crawford, for even in drek like this she gives a performance.

I Saw What You Did

A William Castle Production
for Universal Pictures

(1965)

CAST: Joan Crawford, John Ireland, Leif Erickson, Sara Lane, Andi Garrett, Sharyl Locke, Patricia Breslin, John Archer, John Crawford, Joyce Meadows.

CREDITS: Based on the novel by Ursula Curtiss. Screenplay by William McGivern. Produced and directed by William Castle. Cameraman, Joseph Biroc. Music by Van Alexander. Editor, Edwin H. Bryant. Assistant Director, Terry Morse, Jr. Running time, 82 minutes.

SYNOPSIS

Kit and Libby (Sara Lane and Andi Garrett), two mischievous teen-agers, have been left alone by one of the girls' parents (Leif Erickson and Patricia Breslin) with Libby's younger sister Tess (Sharyl Locke). The house is in an isolated sector. To amuse themselves, the girls concoct a telephone game. They dial a number at random from the phone book, and repeat to whomever answers: "I saw what you did, and I know who you are." It so happens that they eventually say these words to Steve Marak (John Ireland), a neighbor who has just murdered his wife, Judith (Joyce Meadows). Marak decides to track down the girls to silence them, as he is convinced that they are the only "witnesses" to the murder he has just committed. Amy Nelson (Joan Crawford), Marak's next-door neighbor, is in love with him, and has been trying to pirate him away from his wife. When she learns that he is a murderer, she tries to protect the girls, whom he has finally traced via the telephone. Marak then commits his second murder; this time it's Amy, whom he dispatches with a bread knife. Marak closes in on the girls' house, and they grow more and more panic-stricken. But the police and the girls' parents arrive in time to prevent Marak from committing any more homicides.

What the critics said about
I SAW WHAT YOU DID

In Saturday Review

Unfortunately, there is little for eye, ear, or mind in William Castle's egregiously low-budgeted *I Saw What You Did*, an attempt at terror starring Joan Crawford and John Ireland. In point of fact, perhaps for budgetary reasons, Miss Crawford is eliminated by her co-star quite early in the proceedings, before he turns to the more pressing matter of tracking down the source of a phone call that tells him, "I saw what you did and I know who you are"—moments after he has murdered his wife. The call, from teen-age pranksters Andi

Garrett and Sara Lane, probably seemed like a good "gimmick" on which to base an entire film. It isn't.

In Variety

William Castle's *I Saw What You Did* is a well-produced, well-acted entry in the suspense-terror field. . . . Top billing for Miss Crawford is justified only by making allowances for drawing power of her name. But her role as Ireland's shrewish, predatory lover is well handled and vital to the story. Slightest gesture or expression of this veteran thesp conveys vivid emotion.

In the New York Morning Telegraph

So what does all this prove? I dunno, except that *I Saw What You Did* is another of those assembly-line shockers ground out with such regularity by producer William Castle, that Miss Crawford is still as handsome a figure of a woman as she ever was, and that John Ireland makes as menacing a murderer as could be desired.

Berserk

A Herman Cohen Production
for Columbia Pictures

(1968)

CAST: Joan Crawford, Ty Hardin, Diana Dors, Michael Gough, Judy Geeson, Robert Hardy, Geoffrey Keen, Sydney Tafler, George Claydon, Philip Madoc, Ambrostine Phillpotts, Thomas Cimarro, Peter Burton, Golda Casimir, Ted Lune, Milton Reid, Marianne Stone, Miki Iveria, Howard Goorney, Reginald Marsh, Bryan Pringle.

CREDITS: Original story and screenplay by Aben Kandel and Herman Cohen. Producer, Herman Cohen. Directed by Jim O'Connolly. Associate Producer, Robert Sterne. Director of Photography, Desmond Dickinson, B.S.C. Art Director, Maurice Pelling. Costumes by Jay Hutchinson Scott. Wardrobe by Joyce Stoneman. Music composed and conducted by John Scott. Film editor, Raymond Poulton. Running time, 96 minutes.

SYNOPSIS

Monica Rivers (Joan Crawford) is the owner and ringmistress of a traveling English circus. Dressed in leotard, red jacket, and top hat, she herself announces the death-defying acts. A series of mysterious murders begins to occur in the circus. The first to die is Gaspar the Great (Thomas Cimarro), a high-wire walker, who is killed by the breaking of his wire. Investigation reveals that the wire has been cut through. Monica's coldness regarding the event shocks her associates. She even suggests that her business manager and sometime lover, Dorando (Michael Gough), play up the affair for publicity purposes. Dorando, disgusted and disillusioned, decides to abandon the circus, and asks Monica to buy his share. When she refuses, they quarrel. The new high-wire walker, Frank Hawkins (Ty Hardin), arrives, and Monica is impressed when the handsome and muscular Frank tells her he will do his act over a huge bed of vicious spikes. Frank and Monica begin an affair, which arouses Dorando's jealousy. When Dorando is found dead shortly afterward, the people of the circus begin to take alarm, as a mysterious killer is obviously loose in their midst. Many suspect Monica herself, as her cold-blooded, ruthless ways have not made her popular. Frank goes to Monica and tells her that he saw her leaving Dorando's caravan immediately after his death. He then blackmails Monica into giving him a share in the circus. At this point, Monica's unruly, sixteen-year-old daughter, Angela (Judy Geeson), is expelled from a school which has declared her incorrigible. Monica is forced to take her into the circus, and Angela becomes the partner of a knife-thrower named Gustavo (Peter Burton). More tampering with equipment ensues, and then one night Frank is doing his high-wire act when a knife flies through the air and buries itself in his back. He drops into the bed of spikes below. But Deputy Superintendent Brooks (Robert Hardy), one of the London police assigned to cover the circus, has seen the knife-thrower. It is Angela, who over the years had gone insane, it seems, because she felt unloved and neglected while her mother concentrated on business. Angela attempts to kill Monica, but the police intervene. She tries to run away but is struck down by a short-circuit outside the tent and dies in the rain, with the grieving Monica at her side.

What the critics said about BERSERK

Co-player Judy Geeson in Screen Life interview

[Joan was] fabulous, concentrates on her part with fantastic intensity and professionalism.

Howard Thompson in the New York Times

[Miss Crawford] is professional as usual, and certainly the shapeliest ringmaster ever to handle a ring microphone.

Lawrence J. Quirk in Hollywood Screen Parade

Her figure is as trim as ever, her voice as warm and compelling, her legs rival Dietrich's, and her tigress' personality puts to shame most of the mewing kittens who call themselves 1968-style screen actresses. She is all over the picture, radiant, forceful, authoritative, a genuine movie star whose appeal never diminishes.

Frank Leyendecker in Greater Amusements

Joan Crawford gives authority and extreme conviction to the colorful role of a circus owner and ringmaster. . . . As always, Miss Crawford is every inch the glamorous star, this time arrayed in leotard and red-spangled jacket, and she consistently rises above the highly melodramatic, yet exploitable, story material.

With Judy Geeson